CW00321573

STILL STEAMING

A Guide to Britain's Standard Gauge Steam Railways 2006-2007

EDITOR
John Robinson

Tenth Edition

ACKNOWLEDGEMENTS

We were greatly impressed by the friendly and cooperative manner of the staff and helpers of the railways which we selected to appear in this book, and wish to thank them all for the help they have given. In addition we wish to thank Bob Budd (cover design) and Michael Robinson (page layouts) for their help.

Although we believe that the information contained in this guide is accurate at the time of going to press, we, and the Railways and Museums itemised, are unable to accept liability for any loss, damage, distress or injury suffered as a result of any inaccuracies. Furthermore, we and the Railways are unable to guarantee operating and opening times which may always be subject to cancellation without notice.

If you feel we should include other locations or information in future editions, please let us know so that we may give them consideration. We would like to thank you for buying this guide and wish you 'Happy Railway Travelling'!

John Robinson

John Robinson

EDITOR

Note: Further copies of Still Steaming and Little Puffers may be obtained, post free, from our address below or ordered on-line via our web site – www.stillsteaming.com

British Library Cataloguing in Publication Data
A catalogue record for this book is available from the British Library

ISBN-10: 1-86223-140-0
ISBN-13: 978-1-86223-140-5 (for use after January 2007)

Copyright © 2006, MARKSMAN PUBLICATIONS. (01472 696226)
72 St. Peter's Avenue, Cleethorpes, N.E. Lincolnshire, DN35 8HU, England

Manufactured in the UK by LPPS Ltd, Wellingborough, NN8 3PJ

COVER PHOTOGRAPH

We are indebted to photographer Steve Andrews and the Bodmin and Wenford Steam Railway for supplying the cover photo for this book.

This features GWR Prairie 5552 storming up the gradient from Boscarne Junction towards Bodmin.

CONTENTS

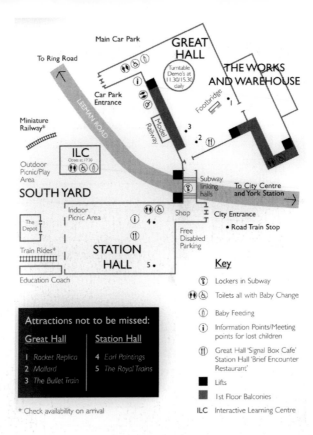

Map labels:
- Main Car Park
- GREAT HALL
- To Ring Road
- THE WORKS AND WAREHOUSE
- Turntable Demo's at 11.30/15.30 daily
- Car Park Entrance
- Footbridge
- Miniature Railway*
- Model Railway
- ILC Closes at 17.30
- Outdoor Picnic/Play Area
- SOUTH YARD
- Subway linking halls
- To City Centre and York Station
- Indoor Picnic Area
- Shop
- City Entrance
- The Depot
- Road Train Stop
- Free Disabled Parking
- Train Rides*
- STATION HALL
- Education Coach

Attractions not to be missed:

Great Hall	Station Hall
1 Rocket Replica	4 Earl Paintings
2 Mallard	5 The Royal Trains
3 The Bullet Train	

* Check availability on arrival

Key

- Lockers in Subway
- Toilets all with Baby Change
- Baby Feeding
- Information Points/Meeting points for lost children
- Great Hall 'Signal Box Cafe' Station Hall 'Brief Encounter Restaurant'
- Lifts
- 1st Floor Balconies
- ILC Interactive Learning Centre

THE FRIENDS OF THE NATIONAL RAILWAY MUSEUM

This organisation was formed in 1977 to help conserve and operate railway exhibits that might otherwise have to wait many years before returning to public view. The organisation is run on a membership basis which imparts a number of privileges which include:

- the *NRM Review*, published quarterly, which keeps Friends in touch with events at the Museum, carries information about the National Collection locomotives, features articles of general railway interest and includes authorative reviews of videos and books.

- opportunities to work as a volunteer in the Museum.

- invitations to FNRM members meetings in York and London.

MEMBERSHIP DETAILS – Normal membership is valid for 12 months from date of registration.

Category	Rate
Ordinary	£20.00
Unwaged	£15.00
Junior (Under 18)	£10.00
Family/Couple	£30.00
Retired Couple	£22.50
Group	£35.00
Life (below 60)	£300.00
Life (60 and over)	£225.00
Life (retired couple)	£350.00
Life (family)	£450.00

Apply for membership to:

FNRM
National Railway Museum
Leeman Road
York
YO26 4XJ

Telephone (01904) 636874
e-mail fnrm@nmsi.ac.uk

Family Membership – is for a maximum of four persons, two or three of whom are under 18 years of age, residing at the same address

Retired Couple Membership – is for two persons aged 60 or over and not in employment.

NATIONAL RAILWAY MUSEUM

Address: National Railway Museum, Leeman Road, York YO26 4XJ	**N° of Steam Locos:** 79
Telephone N°: (01904) 621261	**N° of Other Locos:** 37
Year Formed: 1975	**Approx N° of Visitors P.A.:** 800,000
Location of Line: York	**Web site:** www.nrm.org.uk
Length of Line: Short demonstration line	

GENERAL INFORMATION

Nearest Mainline Station: York (¼ mile)
Nearest Bus Station: York (¼ mile)
Car Parking: On site long stay car park
Coach Parking: On site – free to pre-booked groups
Souvenir Shop(s): Yes
Food & Drinks: Yes

SPECIAL INFORMATION

The Museum is the largest of its kind in the world, housing the Nation's collection of locomotives, carriages, uniforms, posters and an extensive photographic archive. Special events and exhibitions run throughout the year. The Museum is the home of the Mallard – the fastest steam locomotive in the world and Shinkansen, the only Bullet train outside of Japan.

OPERATING INFORMATION

Opening Times: Open daily 10.00am to 6.00pm (closed on 24th, 25th and 26th of December)
Steam Working: School holidays – please phone to confirm details
Prices: Free admission for all (excludes some Special events)
Phone (01904) 686263 for further details.

Detailed Directions by Car:
The Museum is located in the centre of York, just behind the Railway Station. It is clearly signposted from all approaches to York.

Shildon is one of the world's oldest railway towns and was selected by the National Railway Museum as a site for Locomotion, the first national museum to be built in the North East. The new building houses the reserve collection of historically important railway vehicles and these are now accessible to the public for the first time.

Shildon was home to the Timothy Hackworth Museum with its workshops and historic buildings and the incorporation of these with the new Locomotion museum creates an exciting opportunity to discover the significance of Shildon in railway history.

The replica Sans Pareil locomotive pictured below gives rides during the Summer School Holidays and on other special event days.

LOCOMOTION – THE NATIONAL RAILWAY MUSEUM AT SHILDON

Address: Locomotion, Shildon, County Durham   DL14 1PQ
Telephone Nº: (01388) 777999
Year Formed: 2004
Location: Shildon, County Durham
Length of Line: Over ½ mile

Nº of Steam Locos: 60 locomotives and other rail vehicles
Approx Nº of Visitors P.A.: 60,000+
Gauge: Standard
Web site: www.locomotion.uk.com

GENERAL INFORMATION

Nearest Mainline Station: Shildon (adjacent)
Nearest Bus Station: Durham
Car Parking: Available on site
Coach Parking: Available on site
Souvenir Shop(s): Yes
Food & Drinks: Yes

SPECIAL INFORMATION

This extensive site is the first regional branch of the National Railway Museum and houses vehicles from the National Collection in a purpose-built 6,000 square-foot building.

OPERATING INFORMATION

Opening Times: Daily from 7th April 2006 to 31st October 2006 – 10.00am to 5.00pm. Also open from Wednesday to Sunday during the Winter – 10.00am to 4.00pm.
Steam Working: During the Summer School Holidays and on special event days – please phone to confirm details.
Prices: Free admission for all.

Detailed Directions by Car:
From All Parts: Exit the A1(M) at Junction 58 and take the A68 and the A6072 to Shildon. Follow the Brown tourist signs to Locomotion which is situated ¼ mile to the south-east of the Town Centre.

RAILWAY LOCATOR MAP

The numbers shown on this map relate to the page numbers for each railway. Pages 3-5 contain an alphabetical listing of the railways featured in this guide. Please note that the markers on this map show the approximate location only.

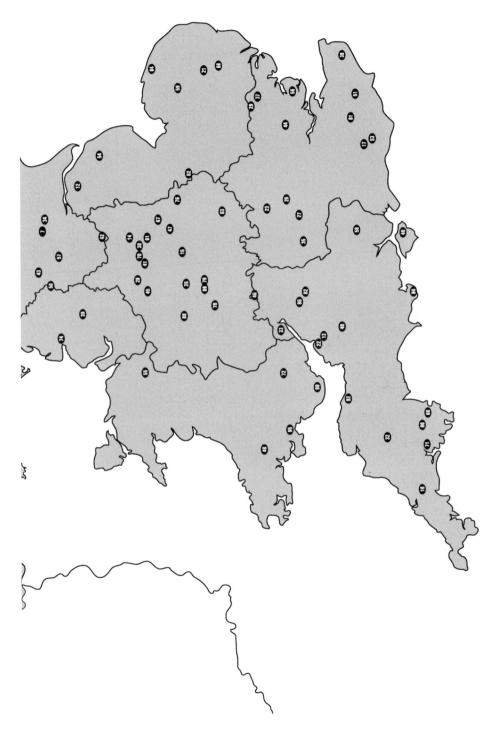

APPLEBY FRODINGHAM RAILWAY

Address: Appleby Frodingham Railway Preservation Society, P.O. Box 44, Brigg, North Lincolnshire DN20 8DW **Telephone Nº**: (01652) 656661 **Year Formed**: 1990 **Location of Line**: Corus Steelworks, Scunthorpe	**Length of Line**: 18 miles of track **Nº of Steam Locos**: 3 **Nº of Other Locos**: 2 **Nº of Members**: 60 **Annual Membership Fee**: – **Gauge**: Standard **Web site**: www.afrps.co.uk

GENERAL INFORMATION

Nearest Mainline Station: Scunthorpe (2 miles)
Nearest Bus Station: Scunthorpe (2 miles)
Car Parking: Large free car park at the site
Coach Parking: At the site
Souvenir Shop(s): Yes – at the Loco Shed
Food & Drinks: Drinks/snacks served on train trips

SPECIAL INFORMATION

A selection of Rail tours and Brake Van tours are operated over a distance of 7 to 18 miles of the steelworks internal railway system.

OPERATING INFORMATION

Opening Times: Selected weekends throughout the year which must be pre-booked via (01652) 657053 or e-mail – bookings@afrps.co.uk
Private Hire of a train is now available for parties and anniveraries with use of the Lounge coach.
Steam Working: See above
Prices: Free – but donations are accepted
Please note that children cannot be carried on Brake van tours due to the open verandahs.

Detailed Directions by Car:
Exit the M180 at Junction 3 onto the M181, at the end turn right onto the A18. Take the 3rd exit at the round-about (still on the A18) and turn left onto Ashby Road at the next roundabout. At the following roundabout turn right into Rowland Road and at the end of the road turn right then left into Entrance E. Car parking is available on the left and the path to the station is on the right.

AVON VALLEY RAILWAY

Address: Bitton Station, Bath Road, Bitton, Bristol BS30 6HD	**No of Steam Locos**: 6
Telephone No: (0117) 932-7296	**No of Other Locos**: 3
Year Formed: 1973	**No of Members**: Approximately 500
Location of Line: Midway between Bristol and Bath on A431	**Annual Membership Fee**: £13.00
	Approx No of Visitors P.A.: 80,000
Length of Line: 3 miles	**Gauge**: Standard
	Web site: www.avonvalleyrailway.org

GENERAL INFORMATION

Nearest Mainline Station: Keynsham (1½ miles)
Nearest Bus Station: Bristol or Bath (7 miles)
Car Parking: Available at Bitton Station
Coach Parking: Available at Bitton Station
Souvenir Shop(s): Yes
Food & Drinks: Yes

SPECIAL INFORMATION

The line has been extended through the scenic Avon Valley towards Bath and a new platform is now open linking with boat trips along the River Avon.

OPERATING INFORMATION

Opening Times: Every Sunday and some Saturdays from Easter to October and on weekends during December. Also Bank Holiday Mondays and Tuesdays to Thursdays during School Holidays. Also open for Santa Specials over Christmas. Open 10.30am to 5.00pm.
Steam Working: 11.00am to 4.00pm
Prices: Adult £5.00
 Child £3.50
 Family Tickets £13.50
 Senior Citizens £4.00

Detailed Directions by Car:
From All Parts: Exit the M4 at Junction 18. Follow the A46 towards Bath and at the junction with the A420 turn right towards Bristol. At Bridge Yate turn left onto the A4175 and continue until you reach the A431. Turn right and Bitton Station is 100 yards on the right.

BARROW HILL ROUNDHOUSE RAILWAY CENTRE

Address: Barrow Hill Roundhouse, Campbell Drive, Barrow Hill, Chesterfield S43 2PR **Telephone Nº**: (01246) 472450 **Year Formed**: 1998 **Location**: Staveley, near Chesterfield **Length of Line**: ¾ mile	**Nº of Steam Locos**: 9 **Nº of Other Locos**: Over 40 **Nº of Members**: Approximately 400 **Annual Membership Fee**: £13.00 Adult **Approx Nº of Visitors P.A.**: 30,000 **Gauge**: Standard **Web site**: www.barrowhill.org.uk

GENERAL INFORMATION

Nearest Mainline Station:
Chesterfield (3½ miles)
Nearest Bus Station:
Chesterfield (3 miles)
Car Parking: Space available for 200 cars
Coach Parking: Available
Souvenir Shop(s): Yes
Food & Drinks: Yes – buffet

SPECIAL INFORMATION

Britain's last remaining operational Railway roundhouse provides storage and repair facilities for standard gauge locomotives and diesels.

OPERATING INFORMATION

Opening Times: Open at weekends throughout the year from 10.00am to 4.30pm (for static viewing).
Steam Working: Special open days only – Real Ale Festival on 19th & 20th May; Special events on 21st & 22nd October and 18th November; Santa Steam Trains on 3rd, 10th and 17th December. Please phone for further details.
Prices: Please phone for prices
Note: Driver training courses are available – please phone for further details.

Detailed Directions by Car:
Exit the M1 at Junction 30 and take the A619 to Staveley (about 3½ miles). Pass through Staveley, turn right at Troughbrook onto 'Works Road'. Continue along for ¾ mile, pass under the railway bridge and take the turn immediately on the right. Turn left onto Campbell Drive and the Roundhouse is behind Acorn Van Hire. The railway is signposted with Brown Tourist signs.

THE BATTLEFIELD LINE

Address: The Battlefield Line,
Shackerstone Station, Shackerstone,
Warwickshire   CV13 6NW
Telephone Nº: (01827) 880754
Year Formed: 1968
Location of Line: North West of Market
Bosworth
Length of Line: 5 miles

Nº of Steam Locos: 5
Nº of Other Locos: 20
Nº of Members: 500 approximately
Annual Membership Fee: £15.00 Adult;
£20.00 Family
Approx Nº of Visitors P.A.: 50,000
Gauge: Standard
Web site: www.battlefield-line-railway.co.uk

GENERAL INFORMATION

Nearest Mainline Station: Nuneaton (9 miles)
Nearest Bus Station: Nuneaton & Hinckley (9 miles)
Car Parking: Ample free parking available
Coach Parking: Can cater for coach parties
Souvenir Shop(s): Yes
Food & Drinks: Yes – Station Buffet

SPECIAL INFORMATION

Travel from the Grade II listed Shackerstone Station
through the beautiful Leicestershire countryside
with views of the adjoining Ashby Canal. Arrive at
the award-winning Shenton Station and explore
Bosworth Battlefield (1485) before making the
return journey.

OPERATING INFORMATION

Operating Info: Weekends and Bank Holidays from
April to October and Santa Specials during
December. Also open on Wednesday afternoons in
July and August. Please telephone for further details.
Opening Times: 10.30am to 6.00pm
Steam Working: From 11.15am to 4.15pm during
high season and Sundays.
Prices: Adult Return £7.00
              Child Return £4.00
              O.A.P. Return £5.00
              Family Ticket £20.00
              (2 adults and 2 children)

Detailed Directions by Car:
Follow the brown tourist signs from the A444 or A447 heading towards the market town of Market Bosworth.
Continue towards the villages of Congerstone & Shackerstone and finally to Shackerstone Station. Access is only
available via the Old Trackbed.

BEAMISH – THE NORTH OF ENGLAND OPEN AIR MUSEUM

Address: Beamish North of England Open Air Museum, Co. Durham DH9 0RG **Telephone N°**: (0191) 370-4000 **Year Formed**: 1970 **Length of Line**: ½ mile	**N° of Steam Locos**: 10 **N° of Other Locos**: 2 **N.B.**: Not all Locos are on display **Approx N° of Visitors P.A.**: 320,000 **Web site**: www.beamish.org.uk

GENERAL INFORMATION

Nearest Mainline Station: Newcastle Central (8 miles); Durham City (12 miles)
Nearest Bus Station: Durham (12 miles), Newcastle (8 miles)
Car Parking: Free parking for 2,000 cars
Coach Parking: Free parking for 40 coaches
Souvenir Shop(s): Yes
Food & Drinks: Yes – self service tea room & licensed period Public House. Coffee shop in Summer.

SPECIAL INFORMATION

A new replica of William Hedley's famous 1813 locomotive "Puffing Billy" is due to enter service at the Pockerley Waggonway at Beamish during late May 2006.

OPERATING INFORMATION

Opening Times: Open all year round: from 10.00am to 4.00pm in the Winter (November to March). Closed on Mondays and Fridays in the Winter. Open from 10.00am to 5.00pm during the Summer (April to October). Check for Christmas opening times.
N.B. Winter visits are centred on the Town and Tramway only. Other areas are closed and admission prices are reduced.
Allow 4-5 hours for a Summer visit and two hours in the Winter.
Steam Working: Daily during the Summer
Prices:
Adult £16.00 in Summer; £6.00 in Winter
Child £10.00 in Summer; £6.00 in Winter
O.A.P. £12.50 in Summer; £6.00 in Winter
Children under 5 are admitted free.
Special Family Tickets are available.

Detailed Directions by Car:
From North & South: Follow the A1(M) to Junction 63 (Chester-le-street) and then take A693 for 4 miles towards Stanley; From North-West: Take the A68 south to Castleside near Consett and follow the signs on the A692 and A693 via Stanley.

THE BLUEBELL RAILWAY

Address: The Bluebell Railway, Sheffield Park Station, Nr. Uckfield, East Sussex, TN22 3QL
Telephone Nº: (01825) 720800
Information Line: (01825) 720825
Year Formed: 1959
Location of Line: Nr. Uckfield, E. Sussex
Length of Line: 9 miles

Nº of Steam Locos: Over 30 with up to 3 in operation on any given day
Nº of Other Locos: –
Nº of Members: 8,000
Annual Membership Fee: £17.00 Adult
Approx Nº of Visitors P.A.: 175,000
Gauge: Standard
Web site: www.bluebell-railway.co.uk

GENERAL INFORMATION

Nearest Mainline Station: East Grinstead (2 miles) with a bus connection
Nearest Bus Station: East Grinstead
Car Parking: Parking at Sheffield Park and Horsted Keynes Stations.
Coach Parking: Sheffield Park is best
Souvenir Shop(s): Yes
Food & Drinks: Yes – buffets and licensed bars & restaurant

SPECIAL INFORMATION

The Railway runs 'Golden Arrow' dining trains on Saturday evenings and Sunday lunchtimes. There is also a museum and model railway at Sheffield Park Station.

OPERATING INFORMATION

Opening Times: Open every weekend throughout the year and also daily from April to October inclusive. Also open during School holidays and for Santa Specials during December. Open from approximately 10.30am to 5.30pm
Steam Working: As above
Prices: Adult Return £9.50
Child Return £4.70
Family Return £27.00 (2 adult + 3 child)
Senior Citizen Return £9.00

Detailed Directions by Car:
Sheffield Park Station is situated on the A275 Wych Cross to Lewes road. Horsted Keynes Station is signposted from the B2028 Lingfield to Haywards Heath road.

BODMIN & WENFORD RAILWAY

Address: Bodmin General Station,
Losthwithiel Road, Bodmin, Cornwall
PL31 1AQ
Telephone Nº: (0845) 1259678
Year Formed: 1984
Location of Line: Bodmin Parkway Station
to Bodmin General & Boscarne Junction.

Length of Line: 6½ miles
Nº of Steam Locos: 10
Nº of Other Locos: 9
Nº of Members: 850
Annual Membership Fee: £12.00
Approx Nº of Visitors P.A.: 51,500
Gauge: Standard

GENERAL INFORMATION

Nearest Mainline Station: Bodmin Parkway
Nearest Bus Station: Bodmin (¼ mile)
Car Parking: Free parking at site
Coach Parking: Free parking at site
Souvenir Shop(s): Yes
Food & Drinks: Yes

SPECIAL INFORMATION

The Railway has steep gradients and there are two
different branches to choose from Bodmin General.
Through tickets to "Bodmin & Wenford Railway" are
available from all Mainline stations.

Web site: www.bodminandwenfordrailway.co.uk

OPERATING INFORMATION

Opening Times: Daily from 27th May to the end of
September. Also daily during Easter week. Open
other selected dates from March to May + October
and also for Santa Specials in December. Open from
10.00am to 5.00pm but also during certain evenings
in the Summer.
Steam Working: Usually trains are steam-hauled
except for most Saturdays when Diesels are used.
Prices: Adult Return £7.50 to £10.00
     Child Return £4.00 to £6.00
     Family Return £21.50 to £28.00
     (2 adults + 2 children)

Detailed Directions by Car:
From the A30/A38 follow the signs to Bodmin Town Centre then follow the brown tourist signs to the Steam
Railway on the B3268 Losthwithiel Road.

BO'NESS & KINNEIL RAILWAY

Address: Bo'ness Station, Union Street, Bo'ness, West Lothian EH51 9AQ	**N° of Steam Locos:** 21
	N° of Other Locos: 18
Telephone N°: (01506) 822298	**N° of Members:** 1,300
Year Opened: 1981	**Annual Membership Fee:** £17.00
Location of Line: Bo'ness to Birkhill	**Approx N° of Visitors P.A.:** 60,000
Length of Line: 3½ miles	**Gauge:** Standard
	Web site: www.srps.org.uk

GENERAL INFORMATION

Nearest Mainline Station: Linlithgow (3 miles)
Nearest Bus Station: Bo'ness (¼ mile)
Car Parking: Free parking at Bo'ness and Birkhill Stations
Coach Parking: Free parking at Bo'ness Station
Souvenir Shop(s): Yes
Food & Drinks: Yes

SPECIAL INFORMATION

The Scottish Railway Exhibition is situated at Bo'ness and conducted tours are also available of the caverns of Birkhill Mine.

OPERATING INFORMATION

Opening Times: Open on weekends from 1st April to 29th October. Also open daily from 1st July to 27th August with diesels only running on Mondays.
Steam Working: The first train leaves at 11.00am and is steam-hauled as are all trains during the day. The last train leaves at 4.15pm and is diesel-hauled.
Prices: Adult Return £5.00   Child Return £2.50
Family Return £13.00   Concession Return £4.00
N.B. Group discounts are also available – please phone for further details. Also, special fares and timetables apply for special events.

Detailed Directions by Car:
From Edinburgh: Take the M9 and exit at Junction 3. Then take the A904 to Bo'ness; From Glasgow: Take the M80 to M876 and then M9 (South). Exit at Junction 5 and take A904 to Bo'ness; From the North: Take M9 (South), exit at Junction 5, then take A904 to Bo'ness; From Fife: Leave the A90 after the Forth Bridge, then take A904 to Bo'ness.

BOWES RAILWAY

Address: Bowes Railway, Springwell Village, Gateshead, Tyne & Wear NE9 7QJ	**N° of Steam Locos:** 2
	N° of Other Locos: 4
Telephone N°: (0191) 416-1847	**N° of Members:** Approximately 70
Year Formed: 1976	**Annual Membership Fee:** £12.00
Location of Line: Springwell Village	**Approx N° of Visitors P.A.:** 5,000
Length of Line: 1¼ miles	**Gauge:** Standard

GENERAL INFORMATION

Nearest Mainline Station: Newcastle Central (3 miles)
Nearest Bus Station: Gateshead Interchange (2 miles)
Car Parking: Free parking at site
Coach Parking: Free parking at site
Souvenir Shop(s): Yes
Food & Drinks: Yes

SPECIAL INFORMATION

Designed by George Stephenson and opened in 1826, the Railway is a scheduled Ancient Monument which operates unique preserved standard gauge rope-hauled inclines and steam hauled passenger trains.

OPERATING INFORMATION

Opening Times: The Springwell site is open for visitors (no charges) on weekdays and some Saturdays throughout the year – 10.00am to 3.00pm.
Steam Working: No trains will run for at least the first half of 2006 as the railway has been closed to operation to allow a major track re-laying campaign to go ahead. Please contact the railway for details of any special events which may be held during the second half of 2006.
Prices: No charges for visting at present although this may change for any special events held in 2006.

Web site: www.bowesrailway.co.uk

Detailed Directions by Car:
From A1 (Northbound): Follow the A194(M) to the Tyne Tunnel and turn left at the sign for Springwell; From A1 (Southbound): Take the turn off left for the B1288 to Springwell and Wrekenton.

BRESSINGHAM STEAM EXPERIENCE

Address: Bressingham Steam Museum, Bressingham, Diss, Norfolk IP22 2AB
Telephone Nº: (01379) 686900
Year Formed: Mid 1950's
Location of Line: Bressingham, Near Diss
Length of Line: 5 miles in total (3 lines)

Nº of Steam Locos: Many Steam locos
Nº of Other Locos: –
Nº of Members: 70 volunteers
Annual Membership Fee: –
Approx Nº of Visitors P.A.: 80,000+
Gauge: Standard & 3 Narrow gauge lines

GENERAL INFORMATION

Nearest Mainline Station: Diss (2½ miles)
Nearest Bus Station: Bressingham (1¼ miles)
Car Parking: Free parking for 400 cars available
Coach Parking: Free parking for 30 coaches
Souvenir Shop(s): Yes
Food & Drinks: Yes

SPECIAL INFORMATION

In addition to Steam locomotives, Bressingham has a large selection of steam traction engines, fixed steam engines and also the National Dad's Army Museum, two extensive gardens and a water garden centre.

Web site: www.bressingham.co.uk

OPERATING INFORMATION

Opening Times: Daily from 24th March to the 30th October 10.30am to 4.30pm. Open until 5.30pm in May, June, July and August.
Steam Working: Almost every operating day except for most Mondays & Tuesdays in April, May, June, July, September and October. Phone for details.
Prices: Adult £8.50 (non-Steam) £12.00 (Steam)
Child £5.00 (non-Steam) £8.00 (Steam)
Family £22 (non-Steam) £35.00 (Steam)
Seniors £7 (non-Steam) £10.00 (Steam)
Steam prices shown are for High Season – Low Season prices with Steam are slightly lower.

Detailed Directions by Car:
From All Parts: Take the A11 to Thetford and then follow the A1066 towards Diss for Bressingham. The Museum is signposted by the brown tourist signs.

BRISTOL HARBOUR RAILWAY

Address: Bristol Industrial Museum, Princes Wharf, City Docks, Bristol, BS1 4RN **Telephone Nº:** (0117) 925-1470 **Year Formed:** 1978 **Location of Line:** South side of the Floating Harbour	**Length of Line:** 1½ miles **Nº of Steam Locos:** 2 **Nº of Other Locos:** 1 **Nº of Members:** – **Annual Membership Fee:** – **Approx Nº of Visitors P.A.:** 70,000 **Gauge:** Standard

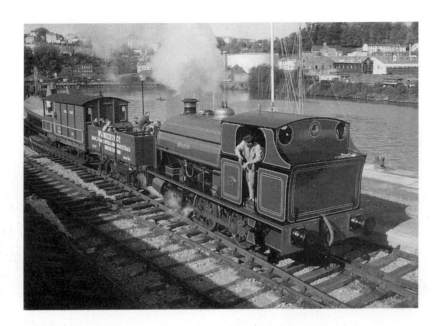

GENERAL INFORMATION

Nearest Mainline Station: Bristol Temple Meads (1 mile)
Nearest Bus Station: City Centre (½ mile)
Car Parking: Parking available at site
Coach Parking: Drop off and Pick up only
Souvenir Shop(s): Yes
Food & Drinks: Cafes available near the Railway

SPECIAL INFORMATION

The Railway is one of the attractions of the Bristol Industrial Museum which has over 400 exhibits to see, housed in historic transit sheds by a dockside location.

OPERATING INFORMATION

Opening Times: Saturday to Wednesday throughout the year. Opens from 10.00am – 5.00pm
Steam Working: 2006 dates: March 25/26; April 1/2/15/16/17/29/30; May 1/13/14/27/28/29; June 10/11/24/25; July 8/9/22/23/29/30; August 12/13/26/27/28; September 9/10/23/24; October 7/8/21/22/28/29.
Prices: Return £1.00 – £2.00 (Depends on length
  Single £0.50 – £1.00   of the journey)
(Children under 6 travel for free)
Note: Admission to the Museum is free of charge.

Detailed Directions by Car:
From All Parts: Follow signs to Bristol City Centre and then the Brown Tourist signs for the Museum. A good landmark to look out for are the 4 huge quayside cranes.

BUCKINGHAMSHIRE RAILWAY CENTRE

Address: Quainton Road Station, Quainton, Aylesbury, Bucks. HP22 4BY	**Nº of Steam Locos**: 30
Telephone Nº: (01296) 655720	**Nº of Other Locos**: 6
Year Formed: 1969	**Nº of Members**: 1,000
Location of Line: At Quainton on the old Metropolitan/Great Central Line	**Annual Membership Fee**: £15.00
	Approx Nº of Visitors P.A.: 40,000
	Gauge: Standard (also a Miniature line)
Length of Line: 2 × ½ mile demo tracks	**Recorded Info. Line**: (01296) 655450

GENERAL INFORMATION

Nearest Mainline Station: Aylesbury (6 miles)
Nearest Bus Station: Aylesbury
Car Parking: Free parking for 500 cars available
Coach Parking: Free parking for 10 coaches
Souvenir Shop(s): Yes
Food & Drinks: Yes

SPECIAL INFORMATION

In addition to a large collection of locomotives and carriages, the Centre has an extensive ½ mile outdoor miniature railway system operated by the Vale of Aylesbury Model Engineering Society.

Web site: www.bucksrailcentre.org

OPERATING INFORMATION

Opening Times: Wednesday to Sunday and Bank Holidays from March to October. Open from 10.30am to 4.30pm.
Steam Working: Sundays and Bank Holidays from April to October and also on Wednesdays during the School holidays.
Prices: Adult £6.50 – £7.50
          Child £4.00 – £5.00
          (Under 5's Free of charge)
          Senior Citizen £5.50 – £6.50
          Family £20.00 – £22.00
          (2 adults + up to 4 children)
Note: Rides on the Miniature Railway cost 60p

Detailed Directions by Car:
The Buckinghamshire Railway Centre is signposted off the A41 Aylesbury to Bicester Road at Waddesdon and off the A413 Buckingham to Aylesbury road at Whitchurch. Junctions 7, 8 and 9 of the M40 are all close by.

CALEDONIAN RAILWAY

Address: The Station, 2 Park Road, Brechin, Angus DD9 7AF
Telephone Nº: (01561) 377760
Year Formed: 1979
Location of Line: From Brechin to the Bridge of Dun
Length of Line: 4 miles

Nº of Steam Locos: 10
Nº of Other Locos: 12
Nº of Members: 250
Annual Membership Fee: Adult £12.00; Family £15.00; OAP/Junior £5.00
Approx Nº of Visitors P.A.: 12,000
Gauge: Standard
Web site: www.caledonianrailway.co.uk

GENERAL INFORMATION

Nearest Mainline Station: Montrose (4½ miles)
Nearest Bus Station: Brechin (200 yards)
Car Parking: Ample free parking at both Stations
Coach Parking: Free parking at both Stations
Souvenir Shop(s): Yes
Food & Drinks: Light refreshments are available

SPECIAL INFORMATION

Brechin Station is the only original Terminus station in preservation.

OPERATING INFORMATION

Opening Times: Easter Sunday, the two weekends before Christmas and every Sunday from 28th May to 3rd September. Also open on 15th, 22nd and 29th July, 12th and 19th August. Contact the railway for details of other Special Events throughout the year.
Steam Working: Steam service on every Sunday.
Prices: Adult Return £5.00
   Child Return £3.00
   Senior Citizen Return £4.00
   Family Return £16.00 (2 adult + 3 child)
Group discounts are available if booked in advance.

Detailed Directions by Car:
From South: For Brechin Station, leave the A90 at the Brechin turn-off and go straight through the Town Centre. Pass the Northern Hotel, take the 2nd exit at the mini-roundabout then it is 150 yards to Park Road/St. Ninian Square; From North: For Brechin Station, leave the A90 at the Brechin turn-off and go straight through Trinity Village. Turn left at the mini-roundabout, it is then 250 yards to Park Road/St. Ninian Square. Bridge of Dun is situated half way between Brechin and Montrose. (Follow tourist signs).

CHASEWATER RAILWAY

Address: Chasewater Country Park, Pool Road, Near Brownhills, Staffs, WS8 7NL **Telephone Nº**: (01543) 452623 **Year Re-formed**: 1985 **Location of Line**: Chasewater Country Park, Brownhills, near Walsall **Length of Line**: 2 miles	**Nº of Steam Locos**: 7 **Nº of Other Locos**: 15 **Nº of Members**: 500 **Annual Membership Fee**: Adult £10.00; Family £15.00; Concessions £7.50 **Approx Nº of Visitors P.A.**: 30,000 **Gauge**: Standard **Web site**: www.chasewaterrailway.co.uk

GENERAL INFORMATION

Nearest Mainline Station: Walsall or Birmingham (both approximately 8 miles)
Nearest Bus Station: Walsall or Birmingham
Car Parking: Free parking in Chasewater Park
Coach Parking: Free parking in Chasewater Park
Souvenir Shop(s): Yes
Food & Drinks: Yes

SPECIAL INFORMATION

Chasewater Railway is based on the Cannock Chase & Wolverhampton Railway opened in 1856. The railway passed into the hands of the National Coal Board which then ceased using the line in 1965. An extension to Chasetown and a new station at Chasewater Heaths is now open as is a new Heritage Centre at Brownhills West.

OPERATING INFORMATION

Opening Times: Sundays and Bank Holiday Mondays throughout the year plus most Saturdays from July to September and Wednesdays from 21st June to 6th September. Also Santa Specials in December. A regular service runs from 11.00am on operating days.
Steam Working: Please phone for details.
Prices: Adult Return £2.95
Child Return £1.95
Family Return £7.45
All tickets offer unlimited rides on the day of issue.

Detailed Directions by Car:
Chasewater Country Park is situated in Brownhills off the A5 southbound near the junction of the A5 with the A452 Chester Road. Follow the Brown tourist signs on the A5 for the Country Park.

CHINNOR & PRINCES RISBOROUGH RAILWAY

Address: Station Road, Chinnor, Oxon	**N° of Steam Locos**: 1
Telephone N°: (01844) 353535 (timetable)	**N° of Other Locos**: 3
Year Formed: 1989	**N° of Members**: 1,000
Location of Line: The Icknield Line, Chinnor	**Annual Membership Fee**: Adult £13.00; Family £20.00; Child £5.00; OAP £8.00
Length of Line: 3½ miles	**Approx N° of Visitors P.A.**: 15,000
Gauge: Standard	**Web Site**: www.cprra.co.uk

Photo courtesy of Peter Harris

GENERAL INFORMATION

Nearest Mainline Station: Princes Risborough (4 miles)
Nearest Bus Station: High Wycombe (10 miles)
Car Parking: Free parking at site
Coach Parking: Prior arrangement preferred but not necessary
Souvenir Shop(s): Yes
Food & Drinks: Soft drinks and light snacks in Station Buffet. Buffet usually available on trains.

SPECIAL INFORMATION

The Chinnor & Princes Risborough Railway operates the remaining 3½ mile section of the former GWR Watlington Branch from Chinnor to Thame Junction.

OPERATING INFORMATION

Opening Times: Sundays from April to October + December and Saturdays during School holidays.
Steam Working: Operates from 10.00am to 5.00pm on Sundays.
Prices: Adult £7.50
    Child £3.75
    Family £19.50 (2 adults + 2 children)
    Senior Citizen £6.50

Detailed Directions by Car:
From All Parts: The railway at Chinnor is situated in Station Road just off the B4009. Junction 6 of the M40 is 4 miles away and Princes Risborough 4 miles further along the B4009. Once in Chinnor follow the brown Tourist signs to the railway.

CHOLSEY & WALLINGFORD RAILWAY

Address: Wallingford Station, 5 Hithercroft Road, Wallingford, Oxon, OX10 9GQ	**N⁰ of Steam Locos**: 1 (+ visiting Locos)
	N⁰ of Other Locos: 4
	N⁰ of Members: 250
Telephone N⁰: (01491) 835067 (24hr info)	**Annual Membership Fee**: £15.00
Year Formed: 1981	**Approx N⁰ of Visitors P.A.**: 6,500
Location of Line: Wallingford, Oxon.	**Gauge**: Standard
Length of Line: 2½ miles	

GENERAL INFORMATION

Nearest Mainline Station: Joint station at Cholsey
Nearest Bus Station: Wallingford (¼ mile)
Car Parking: Off road parking available
Coach Parking: Off road parking available
Souvenir Shop(s): Yes
Food & Drinks: Yes

SPECIAL INFORMATION

The Wallingford branch was originally intended as a through line to Princes Risborough, via Watlington, but became the first standard gauge branch of Brunel's broad-gauge London to Bristol line.

OPERATING INFORMATION

Opening Times: Selected weekends from Easter until Christmas – please phone for further details.
Steam Working: Approximately 11.00am to 4.30pm
Prices: Adult Return £6.00
Child Return £4.00
Concessionary Return £4.50
Family Return £15.50 (2 adult + 3 child)
Prices: Prices are subject to change for Ivor the Engine visits and other special events.

Web site: www.cholsey-wallingford-railway.com

Detailed Directions by Car:
From All Parts: Exit from the A34 at the Milton Interchange (between E. Ilsley and Abingdon). Follow signs to Didcot and Wallingford (A4130). Take Wallingford bypass, then turn left at the first roundabout (signposted Hithercroft Road). The Station is then ½ mile on the right.

CHURNET VALLEY RAILWAY

Address: The Railway Station, Cheddleton, Leek, Staffs. ST13 7EE	**N° of Steam Locos:** 2
Telephone N°: (01538) 360522	**N° of Other Locos:** 3
Year Formed: 1978	**N° of Members:** –
Location of Line: Cheddleton to Froghall	**Annual Membership Fee:** £14.00
Length of Line: 5½ miles	**Approx N° of Visitors P.A.:** 58,000
	Gauge: Standard
	Web site: www.churnetvalleyrailway.co.uk

GENERAL INFORMATION

Nearest Mainline Station: Stoke-on-Trent (12 miles)
Nearest Bus Station: Leek (5 miles)
Car Parking: Parking available on site
Coach Parking: Restricted space – please book in advance
Souvenir Shop(s): Yes
Food & Drinks: Yes

SPECIAL INFORMATION

Cheddleton Station is a Grade II listed building, Consall is a sleepy halt with Victorian charm, whereas Kingsley & Froghall are new NSR-style buildings with disabled and tearoom facilities.

OPERATING INFORMATION

Opening Times: Weekends from March to October. Wednesdays in June, July and August and also Bank Holiday Mondays. A Diesel service runs daily throughout August and a Steam service runs on Wednesdays in June, July and August. Please phone for details of other services.
Steam Working: Please phone for a timetable.
Prices: Please telephone (01538) 360522 for details.

Detailed Directions by Car:
From All Parts: Take the M6 to Stoke-on-Trent and follow trunk roads to Leek. Cheddleton Station is just off the A520 Leek to Stone road. Kingsley & Froghall Station is just off the A52 Ashbourne Road.

COLNE VALLEY RAILWAY

Address: Castle Hedingham Station, Yeldham Road, Castle Hedingham, Essex, CO9 3DZ
Telephone Nº: (01787) 461174
Year Formed: 1974
Location of Line: On A1017, 7 miles north-west of Braintree
Length of Line: Approximately 1 mile

Nº of Steam Locos: 10
Nº of Other Locos: 11
Nº of Members: 280
Annual Membership Fee: £11.00
Approx Nº of Visitors P.A.: 45,000
Gauge: Standard
Web Site: www.colnevalleyrailway.co.uk

GENERAL INFORMATION

Nearest Mainline Station: Braintree (7 miles)
Nearest Bus Station: Hedingham bus from Braintree stops at the Railway (except on Sundays)
Car Parking: Parking at the site
Coach Parking: Free parking at site
Souvenir Shop(s): Yes
Food & Drinks: Yes – on operational days. Also Pullman Sunday Lunches – bookings necessary.

SPECIAL INFORMATION

The railway is being re-built on a section of the old Colne Valley & Halstead Railway, with all buildings, bridges, signal boxes, etc. re-located on site.
The Railway also has a Farm Park to visit on site (open between 1st May and 24th September only).

OPERATING INFORMATION

Opening Times: Trains run every Sunday and Bank Holiday weekend from 14th April to 8th October. Open daily in August except for Mondays and Fridays. Pre-booked parties any time by arrangement and various other special events.
Steam Working: Sundays 12.00pm to 4.00pm. Also Wednesdays in August 11.30am–3.30pm.
Prices: Adult – Steam days £6.00; Diesel £5.00
Child – Steam £3.00; Diesel £2.50
Family (2 adults + 4 children) –
Steam £20.00; Diesel £16.00

Detailed Directions by Car:
The Railway is situated on the A1017 between Halstead and Haverhill, 7 miles north-west of Braintree.

CRICH TRAMWAY VILLAGE

Address: Crich Tramway Village, Crich, Matlock, Derbyshire DE4 5DP	**N° of Steam Locos**: None
Telephone N°: (01773) 854321	**N° of Other Locos**: 50 trams approx.
Year Formed: 1964	**N° of Members**: 2,500
Location of Line: Crich	**Annual Membership Fee**: £20.00
Length of Line: 1 mile	**Approx N° of Visitors P.A.**: 100,000
	Web site: www.tramway.co.uk

GENERAL INFORMATION

Nearest Mainline Station: Whatstandwell (1 mile)
Nearest Bus Station: Crich
Car Parking: Free parking available on site
Coach Parking: Free parking available on site
Souvenir Shop(s): Yes
Food & Drinks: Yes

SPECIAL INFORMATION

The admission price includes unlimited tram rides plus a host of indoor attractions.

OPERATING INFORMATION

Opening Times: 10.30am to 4.00pm daily from 11th to26th February and in weekends in March. Open daily from 1st April to 29th October 10.00am to 5.30pm then weekends in November and December from 10.30am to 4.00pm.
Steam Working: On certain Special event days only – please phone for details.
Prices: Adult £9.00
         Child £4.50
         Senior Citizen £8.00
         Family Tickets £24.00

Detailed Directions by Car:
From All Parts: The Museum is situated just of the B5035 near Crich – this is approximately 15 miles north of Derby. Exit the M1 at Junction 28 if travelling from the North or Junction 26 from the South.

DARLINGTON RAILWAY CENTRE & MUSEUM

Address: North Road Station, Darlington,
Co. Durham DL3 6ST
Telephone N°: (01325) 460532
Year Formed: 1975
Location of Line: Adjacent to North
Road Station
Length of Line: ¼ mile

N° of Steam Locos: 5
N° of Other Locos: –
N° of Members: –
Annual Membership Fee: –
Approx N° of Visitors P.A.: 27,091
Gauge: Standard
Web site: www.drcm.org.uk

GENERAL INFORMATION

Nearest Mainline Station: North Road (adjacent)
Nearest Bus Station: Darlington (1 mile)
Car Parking: Free parking at site
Coach Parking: Free parking at site
Souvenir Shop(s): Yes
Food & Drinks: Cafe open 11.00am to 3.00pm.
Drinks machine and confectionery at other times.

SPECIAL INFORMATION

The museum is an 1842 station on the route of the
Stockton and Darlington Railway and is devoted to
the Railways of north-east England.

OPERATING INFORMATION

Opening Times: The Museum is open 10.00am to
5.00pm daily except Christmas Day, Boxing Day and
New Year's Day.
The Locomotive Works run by the A1 Steam
Locomotive Trust is usually open on the 2nd
Saturday of each month.
Steam Working: At various Special events
throughout the year – please phone for details.
Prices: Adult £2.50
Child £1.50
Senior Citizen £1.50
Family Ticket £7.50

Detailed Directions by Car:
From Darlington Town Centre: Follow the A167 north for about ¾ mile then turn left immediately before the
Railway bridge; From A1(M): Exit at Junction 59 then follow A167 towards Darlington and turn right after
passing under the Railway bridge.

THE DARTMOOR RAILWAY

Address: Okehampton Station, Station Road, Okehampton   EX20 1EH
Telephone Nº: (01837) 55637
Year Formed: 1997
Location of Line: Sampford Courtenay to Meldon Quarry
Length of Line: 15 miles

Nº of Steam Locos: None – but visits from Steam locos are planned
Nº of Other Locos: 3 and DMUs
Gauge: Standard
Web site: www.dartmoorrailway.co.uk

GENERAL INFORMATION

Nearest Mainline Station: Crediton
Nearest Bus Station: Okehampton
Car Parking: Okehampton Station
Coach Parking: Okehampton Station
Souvenir Shop(s): Yes
Food & Drinks: Daily from 10.00am to 3.00pm

SPECIAL INFORMATION

The Dartmoor Railway operates on the route of the older Southern Railway line from Crediton to Okehampton and Meldon Quarry. Devon Belle Pullman Coaches are used on some services giving the chance to enjoy a meal as the train travels through the National Park. Bicycle hire is available from Okehampton Station.

OPERATING INFORMATION

Opening Times: Open daily from 10.00am to 3.00pm on most days. Open until 5.00pm on days when trains are running.
Steam Working: None at present but planned for later in 2006 if possible. Other services run on weekends and some other dates from 10.00am. Trains run through from Exeter on Sundays during the summer. Phone for further details.
Prices: Adult Return £6.00
     Child Return £3.00

Detailed Directions by Car:
From All Parts: Take the A30 Exeter to Launceston Road to the Okehampton turn-off and follow signs up the hill to the railway station.

DEAN FOREST RAILWAY

Address: Norchard Centre, Forest Road; Lydney, Gloucestershire GL15 4ET **Telephone Nº**: (01594) 845840 **Information Line**: (01594) 843423 (24 hr.) **Year Formed**: 1970 **Location of Line**: Lydney, Gloucestershire **Length of Line**: 4½ miles	**Nº of Steam Locos**: 7 (2 working) **Nº of Other Locos**: 18 **Nº of Members**: 880 **Annual Membership Fee**: Adult £13.00; Family (4 persons) £16.00 **Approx Nº of Visitors P.A.**: 55,000 **Gauge**: Standard

GENERAL INFORMATION

Nearest Mainline Station: Lydney (200 metres)
Nearest Bus Station: Lydney (1 mile)
Car Parking: 600 spaces available at Norchard
Coach Parking: Ample space available
Souvenir Shop(s): Yes + a Museum
Food & Drinks: Yes – on operational days only

SPECIAL INFORMATION

Dean Forest Railway preserves the sole surviving line of the Severn and Wye Railway. The Railway has lengthened the line to a total of 4½ miles and Norchard to Parkend is now open for steam train operation giving a round trip of 9 miles.

OPERATING INFORMATION

Opening Times: Norchard is open every day for viewing. Trains operate on Sundays from the end of March to the end of October. Also on Wednesdays and Saturdays from June to September and on various other dates. Please phone for further details if required.

Steam Working: Most services are steam-hauled – phone for details. Trains depart Norchard at various times from 10.55am to 3.30pm.

Prices: Adult Return £7.50
Child Return £5.00 (ages 5-16 years old)
Senior Citizens £7.00

N.B. Fares may differ on special dates.

Web site: www.deanforestrailway.co.uk

Detailed Directions by Car:
From M50 & Ross-on-Wye: Take the B4228 and B4234 via Coleford to reach Lydney. Norchard is located on the B4234, ¾ mile north of Lydney Town Centre; From Monmouth: Take the A4136 and B4431 onto the B4234 via Coleford; From South Wales: Take the M4 then M48 onto the A48 via Chepstow to Lydney; From Midlands/Gloucester: Take the M5 to Gloucester then the A48 to Lydney; From the West Country: Take the M4 and M48 via the 'Old' Severn Bridge to Chepstow and then the A48 to Lydney.

DERWENT VALLEY LIGHT RAILWAY

Address: Murton Park, Murton Lane, Murton, York YO19 5UF	**N⁰ of Steam Locos**: 2
Telephone N⁰: (01904) 489966	**N⁰ of Other Locos**: 5
Year Formed: 1991	**N⁰ of Members**: 80
Location of Line: Murton, near York	**Annual Membership Fee**: £10.00
Length of Line: ½ mile	**Approx N⁰ of Visitors P.A.**: 15,000
	Gauge: Standard

GENERAL INFORMATION

Nearest Mainline Station: York (4 miles)
Nearest Bus Station: York (4 miles)
Car Parking: Large free car park at the site
Coach Parking: Free at the site
Souvenir Shop(s): Yes – at the Yorkshire Museum of Farming (same site)
Food & Drinks: Yes – as above

SPECIAL INFORMATION

The site is the remnants of the Derwent Valley Railway which was the last privately owned railway in England, originally opened in 1913.

OPERATING INFORMATION

Opening Times: Sundays and Bank Holidays from Easter until the end of September. Also Santa Specials run in December.
Steam Working: Second and last Sunday in the month and Bank Holidays – 10.30am to 4.30pm.
Prices: Adult £5.00
 Child £3.00
 Senior Citizens/Students £4.00
 Family Tickets £12.00 (2 adult + 4 child)
Prices are for entrance to the Yorkshire Museum of Farming – train rides are included in the price.

Detailed Directions by Car:
From All Parts: The railway is well signposted for the Yorkshire Museum of Farming from the A64 (York to Scarborough road), the A1079 (York to Hull road) and the A166 (York to Bridlington road).

DIDCOT RAILWAY CENTRE

Address: Didcot Railway Centre, Didcot, Oxfordshire OX11 7NJ **Telephone Nº**: (01235) 817200 **Year Formed**: 1961 **Location of Line**: Didcot **Length of Line**: ¾ mile **Gauge**: Standard and 7 foot ¼ inch	**Nº of Steam Locos**: 23 **Nº of Other Locos**: 2 **Nº of Members**: 4,400 **Annual Membership Fee**: Full £24.00; Over 60/Under 18 £16.00; Family £30.00 **Approx Nº of Visitors P.A.**: 70,000 **Web Site**: www.didcotrailwaycentre.org.uk

GENERAL INFO

Nearest Mainline Station:
Didcot Parkway (adjacent)
Nearest Bus Station: Buses to Didcot
call at the Railway station
Car Parking: BR car park adjacent
Coach Parking: Further details on
application
Souvenir Shop(s): Yes
Food & Drinks: Yes

SPECIAL INFO

The Centre is based on a Great Western
Railway engine shed and is devoted to
the re-creation of part of the GWR
including Brunel's broad gauge railway
and a newly built replica of the Fire Fly
locomotive of 1840.

OPERATING INFO

Opening Times: Weekends all year
round, open daily during most school
holidays and then from 24th June to
3rd September. Weekends and Steam
days open 10.00am to 5.00pm. Other
days and during Winter open 10.00am
to 4.00pm.
Steam Working: All Weekends and
Bank Holidays from 29th April to 3rd
September. Wednesdays from 5th July
to 30th August. Phone for details of
Autumn steam days or alternatively
check the web site.
Prices: Adult £4.00–£9.50
           Child £3.00–£7.50
Discounted family tickets are often
available (2 adults + 2 children).
Prices vary depending on the events.

Detailed Directions by Car:
From East & West: Take the M4 to Junction 13 then the A34 and A4130 (follow brown Tourist signs to Didcot
Railway Centre); From North: The centre is signed from the A34 to A4130.

DOWNPATRICK & COUNTY DOWN RAILWAY

Address: Market Street, Downpatrick, Co. Down, Northern Ireland	**Nº of Steam Locos:** 3
Telephone Nº: (07790) 802049	**Nº of Other Locos:** 5
Year Formed: 1985	**Nº of Members:** 180
Location of Line: Downpatrick	**Annual Membership Fee:** Adult £15.00, Family £20.00, Concessions £10.00
Length of Line: 2 miles	**Approx Nº of Visitors P.A.:** 13,000
Gauge: Irish Standard (5 foot 3 inches)	**Web:** www.downrail.co.uk

GENERAL INFORMATION

Nearest Mainline Station: –
Nearest Bus Station: Adjacent to Station
Car Parking: Ample parking adjacent to Station
Coach Parking: Ample parking adjacent to Station
Souvenir Shop(s): Yes
Food & Drinks: Yes

SPECIAL INFORMATION

This is the only operating Standard (5' 3") Gauge Heritage Railway in Ireland.

OPERATING INFORMATION

Opening Times: The Museum is open daily from June to September.
Steam Working: Weekends in June, July, August and also first 2 Saturdays and Sundays in September. Trains are usually steam hauled and run from 2.00pm to 5.00pm. Special trains run at Easter, Halloween and Christmas.
Prices: Adult Return £4.50 (Single £3.00)
     Child Return £3.50 (Single £2.50)

Detailed Directions by Car:
From Belfast take the A7 Downpatrick Road. Upon arrival in Downpatrick, follow the brown tourist signs and the Railway Museum is adjacent to the bus station.

EAST ANGLIAN RAILWAY MUSEUM

Address: Chappel & Wakes Colne
Station, Colchester, Essex   CO6 2DS
Telephone Nº: (01206) 242524
Year Formed: 1969
Location of Line: 6 miles west of
Colchester on Marks Tey to Sudbury branch
Length of Line: A third of a mile

Nº of Steam Locos: 8   **Other Locos**: 4
Nº of Members: 750
Annual Membership Fee: Adult £20.00;
Senior Citizen £15.00
Approx Nº of Visitors P.A.: 40,000
Gauge: Standard
Web site: www.earm.co.uk

GENERAL INFORMATION

Nearest Mainline Station: Chappel & Wakes Colne
(adajcent)
Nearest Bus Stop: Chappel (400 yards)
Car Parking: Free parking at site
Coach Parking: Free parking at site
Souvenir Shop(s): Yes
Food & Drinks: Yes – drinks are available every day
and snacks are also available on operating days.

SPECIAL INFORMATION

The museum has the most comprehensive collection
of railway architecture & engineering in the region.
The railway also has a miniature railway that usually
operates on steam days.

OPERATING INFORMATION

Opening Times: Open daily 10.00am to 5.00pm.
Steam days open from 11.00am to 5.00pm
Steam Working: Steam days are held every month
from April to August and also in October and
December. Bank Holidays are also Steam days.
Check the web site for further details.
Prices: Adult £3.00 non-Steam; £6.00 Steam
Child £2.00 non-Steam; £3.00 Steam
O.A.P. £2.50 non-Steam; £4.50 Steam
Family £8.00 non-Steam; £15.00 Steam
Children under the age of 4 are admitted free of
charge. A 10% discount is available for bookings for
more than 10 people.

Detailed Directions by Car:
From North & South: Turn off the A12 south west of Colchester onto the A1124 (formerly the A604). The
Museum is situated just off the A1124; From West: Turn off the A120 just before Marks Tey (signposted).

EAST KENT RAILWAY

Address: Station Road, Shepherdswell, Dover, Kent CT15 7PD	**No of Steam Locos**: 1
Telephone No: (01304) 832042	**No of Other Locos**: 7 + 2 DMUs
Year Formed: 1985	**No of Members**: 400
Location of Line: Between Shepherdswell and Eythorne	**Annual Membership Fee**: £15.00 (Adult)
Length of Line: 2 miles	**Approx No of Visitors P.A.**: 15,000
	Gauge: Standard and also 5 inch and 3¼ inch miniature gauge

GENERAL INFORMATION

Nearest Mainline Station: Shepherdswell (50 yards)
Car Parking: Available Shepherdswell and Eythorne
Coach Parking: In adjacent Station Yard
Souvenir Shop(s): Yes
Food & Drinks: Yes

SPECIAL INFORMATION

The East Kent Railway was originally built between 1911 and 1917 to service Tilmanstone Colliery. Closed in the mid-1980's, the railway was re-opened in 1995.

OPERATING INFORMATION

Opening Times: Open weekends throughout the year for static viewing from 11.00am to 3.00pm. Trains run during Easter and Sundays from May to September and also weekends in December.
Steam Working: None at present.
Prices: Adult £5.00
               Child £3.50
               Senior Citizens £4.00

Web site: www.eastkentrailway.com

Detailed Directions by Car:
From the A2: Take the turning to Shepherdswell and continue to the village. Pass the shop on the left and cross the railway bridge. Take the next left (Station Road) signposted at the traffic lights for the EKR; From the A256: Take the turning for Eythorne at the roundabout on the section between Eastry and Whitfield. Follow the road through Eythorne. Further on you will cross the railway line and enter Shepherdswell. After a few hundred yards take the right turn signposted for the EKR.

EAST LANCASHIRE RAILWAY

Address: Bolton Street Station, Bury, Lancashire   BL9 0EY
Telephone Nº: (0161) 764-7790
Year Formed: 1968
Location of Line: Heywood, Bury and Rawtenstall
Length of Line: 12 miles

Nº of Steam Locos: 14
Nº of Other Locos: 16
Nº of Members: 4,500
Annual Membership Fee: £14.00
Approx Nº of Visitors P.A.: 110,000
Gauge: Standard
Web site: www.east-lancs-rly.co.uk

GENERAL INFORMATION

Nearest Mainline Station: Manchester (then Metro Link to Bury)
Nearest Bus Station: ¼ mile
Car Parking: Adjacent
Coach Parking: Adjacent
Souvenir Shop(s): Yes
Food & Drinks: Yes

SPECIAL INFORMATION

Originally opened in 1846, the East Lancashire Railway was re-opened in 1991.

OPERATING INFORMATION

Opening Times: Every weekend & Bank Holiday 9.00am to 5.00pm. Also Wednesday to Friday from May to September inclusive. A number of special events also run throughout the year.
Steam Working: Most trains are steam-hauled. Saturdays alternate Steam & Diesel. 2 engines in steam on Sundays.
Prices: Adult Return £10.60
　　　　　　Child Return £7.20
　　　　　　Family Return £28.00
Cheaper fares are available for shorter journeys.

Detailed Directions by Car:
From All Parts: Exit the M66 at Junction 2 and take the A56 into Bury. Follow the brown tourist signs and turn right into Bolton Street at the junction with the A58. The station is about 150 yards on the right.

EAST SOMERSET RAILWAY (STRAWBERRY LINE)

Address: Cranmore Railway Station, Shepton Mallet, Somerset BA4 4QP
Telephone Nº: (01749) 880417
Year Formed: 1971
Location of Line: Cranmore, off A361 between Frome and Shepton Mallet
Length of Line: 3 miles

Nº of Steam Locos: 5
Nº of Other Locos: 2
Nº of Members: 480
Annual Membership Fee: Single £14.00; Couple £18.00; Family £27.00
Approx Nº of Visitors P.A.: 20,000
Gauge: Standard

GENERAL INFORMATION

Nearest Mainline Station: Castle Cary (10 miles)
Nearest Bus Station: Shepton Mallet (3 miles)
Car Parking: Space for 100 cars available
Coach Parking: Available by arrangement
Souvenir Shop(s): Yes
Food & Drinks: Yes

SPECIAL INFORMATION

Footplate experience courses available – phone (01749) 880417 for further details.

Web site: www.eastsomersetrailway.com

OPERATING INFORMATION

Opening Times: Complex, Museum and Engine Sheds open daily except for 25th and 26th December and throughout January and February.
Steam Working: Sundays in the Winter, weekends and bank holidays in April, May & October plus some weekdays in the Summer. Santa Specials run on weekends in December. Other special events run on various dates. Open 10.00am to 4.00pm in the Winter, 10.00am to 5.30pm in the Summer.
Prices: Adults £6.00   Children £4.00
Senior Citizens £5.00
Family £17.00

Detailed Directions by Car:
From the North: Take A367/A37 to Shepton Mallet then turn left onto A361 to Frome. Carry on to Shepton Mallet and 9 miles after Frome turn left at Cranmore; From the South: Take A36 to Frome bypass then A361 to Cranmore; From the West: Take A371 from Wells to Shepton Mallet, then A361 to Frome (then as above).

ECCLESBOURNE VALLEY RAILWAY

Address: Station Road, Coldwell Street, Wirksworth   DE4 4FB
Telephone N°: (01629) 823076
Year Formed: 2000
Location of Line: Wirksworth to Duffield
Length of Line: 1½ miles

N° of Steam Locos: 2
N° of Other Locos: 5
N° of Members: 500+
Annual Membership Fee: £12.00
Approx N° of Visitors P.A.: 10,000
Gauge: Standard
Web site: www.e-v-r.com

GENERAL INFORMATION

Nearest Mainline Station: Cromford (2 miles)
Nearest Bus Station: Derby (13 miles)
Car Parking: Available at the Station
Coach Parking: Available at the Station
Souvenir Shop(s): Yes
Food & Drinks: Yes

SPECIAL INFORMATION

The line is being restored section by section with a view to completing all 8½ miles by 2008.

OPERATING INFORMATION

Opening Times: Daily (except for Christmas Day) from 10.00am to 4.00pm
Steam Working: 3rd and 4th September
Prices: Adult Tickets £3.50 (travel all day)
Child Tickets £1.50 (travel all day)
Concessions Tickets £2.50 (travel all day)

Detailed Directions by Car:
From All Parts: Exit the M1 at Junction 26 and take the A610 Ambergate then the A6 to Whatstandwell. Turn left onto the B5035 to Wirksworth and the station is at the bottom of the hill as you enter the town.

ELSECAR RAILWAY

Address: Wath Road, Elsecar, Barnsley, S74 8HJ	**No of Steam Locos**: 4
Telephone No: (01226) 746746	**No of Other Locos**: 3
Year Formed: –	**No of Members**: –
Location of Line: Elsecar, near Barnsley	**Annual Membership Fee**: £10.00
Length of Line: 1 mile	**Approx No of Visitors P.A.**: –
	Gauge: Standard
	Web site: www.elsecarrailway.cjb.net

GENERAL INFORMATION

Nearest Mainline Station: Elsecar
Nearest Bus Station: Barnsley
Car Parking: Large free car park at the site
Coach Parking: At the site
Souvenir Shop(s): Yes
Food & Drinks: Yes

SPECIAL INFORMATION

The Railway is based at the Elsecar Heritage Centre which is an antiques and craft centre with a wide range of displays and special events.

OPERATING INFORMATION

Opening Times: Heritage centre is open daily from 10.00am to 5.00pm throughout the year except from 25th December to 2nd January.
Steam Working: Trains run on Sundays from March to October – hourly from 12.00pm to 4.00pm and on special event days. Please phone for details.
Prices: Adult £2.50
Senior Citizens/Under 13's £1.00
Admission to the museum and site is free of charge except for the Living History Centre and during Special Events.

Detailed Directions by Car:
From All Parts: Exit the M1 at Junction 36 and follow the brown 'Elsecar Heritage' signs taking the A6135 for approximately 2 miles. Turn left onto Broad Carr Road for just under a mile, then right onto Armroyd Lane and right again onto Fitzwilliam Street. Free visitor car parking is available on Wentworth Road off the junction of Fitzwilliam Street and Wath Road.

EMBSAY & BOLTON ABBEY STEAM RAILWAY

Address: Bolton Abbey Station, Bolton Abbey, Skipton, N. Yorkshire BD23 6AF	**Nº of Steam Locos**: 21
Telephone Nº: (01756) 710614	**Nº of Other Locos**: 11
Year Formed: 1968	**Nº of Members**: 700
Location of Line: 2 miles east of Skipton	**Annual Membership Fee**: £10.00
Length of Line: 4½ miles	**Approx Nº of Visitors P.A.**: 107,000
	Gauge: Standard

GENERAL INFORMATION

Nearest Mainline Station: Skipton (2 miles), Ilkley (3 miles)
Nearest Bus Station: Skipton (2 miles), Ilkley (3 mls)
Car Parking: Large car park at both Stations
Coach Parking: Large coach park at both Stations
Souvenir Shop(s): Yes
Food & Drinks: Yes – Cafe + Buffet cars

SPECIAL INFORMATION

The line extension to Bolton Abbey opened in 1998.

Web site: www.embsayboltonabbeyrailway.org.uk

OPERATING INFORMATION

Opening Times: Every Sunday throughout the year. Weekends from Easter to the end of October and daily in the summer season. Tuesdays in June and September.
Steam Working: Trains depart Embsay Station at 10.30am, 12.00pm, 1.30pm, 3.00pm and 4.30pm during the Main Season. Mondays and Wednesdays are operated by a D.M.U.
Prices: Adult Return £6.00
Child Return £3.00
Family Ticket £16.00 (2 adult + 2 children)
Different fares may apply on special event days.

Detailed Directions by Car:
From All Parts: Embsay Station is off the A59 Skipton bypass by the Harrogate Road. Bolton Abbey Station is off the A59 at Bolton Abbey.

EPPING ONGAR RAILWAY

Address: Ongar Station, Ongar, Essex, CM5 9BN
Telephone Nº: (01277) 366616
Year Formed: 2004
Location of Line: Epping to Ongar
Length of Line: 6 miles

Nº of Steam Locos: 5 (none in steam)
Nº of Other Locos: 4
Nº of Members: None
Annual Membership Fee: –
Approx Nº of Visitors P.A.: 60,000
Gauge: Standard gauge and also 5 feet
Web site: www.eorailway.co.uk

GENERAL INFORMATION

Nearest Mainline Station: Harlow (10 miles)
Nearest Bus Station: Epping (8 miles)
Car Parking: Limited free parking at Ongar and North Weald stations. Parking is available at the London Underground station in Epping with a free Vintage bus link to North Weald.
Coach Parking: By arrangement only
Souvenir Shop(s): Yes
Food & Drinks: Available

SPECIAL INFORMATION

The Railway has 5 Finnish locomotives on display which unfortunately are not able to use the line due to their 5 foot gauge.

OPERATING INFORMATION

Opening Times: Sundays only throughout the year. 11.00am to 3.00pm during the Winter then open until 4.00pm during the Summer.
Steam Working: None at present
Prices: Adult £5.00
Child £3.00 (Under-5s travel free)
Concessions £3.00
Family £12.00 (2 adults + 3 children)

Detailed Directions by Car:
For North Weald Station: Exit the M11 at Junction 7 and follow the A414 towards Chelmsford and North Weald. Take the 3rd exit at the 2nd roundabout ('The Talbot' pub on the left) and follow the road into North Weald village. Station Road is on the left just after leaving the village. For Ongar Station: Exit the M11 at Junction 7 and follow the A414 towards Chelmsford and North Weald. Follow the road for approximately 5 miles going straight on at two roundabouts. At the 3rd roundabout (BP garage on the left) take the third exit towards Ongar. Epping Ongar Railway is located approximately on the right hand side after approximately 400 yards.
At present there is no connection at the Epping end of the line but parking is available at the London Underground Station in Epping and a vintage bus connects with the line at North Weald.

FOXFIELD STEAM RAILWAY

Address: Caverswall Road Station, Blythe Bridge, Stoke-on-Trent, Staffs. ST11 9EA
Telephone Nº: (01782) 396210
Year Formed: 1967
Location of Line: Blythe Bridge
Length of Line: 3½ miles
Gauge: Standard

Nº of Steam Locos: 16
Nº of Other Locos: 15
Nº of Members: Over 300
Annual Membership Fee: Adult £8.00; Junior £5.00; Family £12.00
Approx Nº of Visitors P.A.: 25,000
Web site: www.foxfieldrailway.co.uk

GENERAL INFORMATION

Nearest Mainline Station: Blythe Bridge (¼ mile)
Nearest Bus Station: Hanley (5 miles)
Car Parking: Space for 300 cars available
Coach Parking: Space for 6 coaches available
Souvenir Shop(s): Yes
Food & Drinks: Yes – Buffet and Real Ale Bar

SPECIAL INFORMATION

The Railway is a former Colliery railway built in 1893 to take coal from Foxfield Colliery. It has the steepest Standard Gauge adhesion worked gradient in the UK and freight trains can be seen on these gradients during the annual Steam Gala in July.

OPERATING INFORMATION

Opening Times: Sundays & Bank Holiday Mondays from 2nd April to the end of October. Also weekends in December. Open 10.30am to 5.00pm.
Steam Working: 11.30am, 1.00pm, 2.00pm, 3.00pm & 4.00pm although Special Event days run earlier also.
Prices: Adult Tickets – £6.00
Child Tickets – £4.00
Senior Citizen Tickets – £5.00
Family Tickets – £15.00
Fares may vary on special event days.

Detailed Directions by Car:
From South: Exit M6 at Junction 14 onto the A34 to Stone then the A520 to Meir and the A50 to Blythe Bridge; From North: Exit M6 at Junction 15 then the A500 to Stoke-on-Trent and the A50 to Blythe Bridge; From East: Take the A50 to Blythe Bridge. Once in Blythe Bridge, turn by the Mainline crossing.

GLOUCESTERSHIRE WARWICKSHIRE RAILWAY

Address: The Station, Toddington, Cheltenham, Gloucestershire GL54 5DT	**Nº of Steam Locos:** 11
Telephone Nº: (01242) 621405	**Nº of Other Locos:** 17
Year Formed: 1981	**Nº of Members:** 2,650
Location of Line: 5 miles south of Broadway, Worcestershire, near the A46	**Annual Membership Fee:** £12.00 (Adult)
	Approx Nº of Visitors P.A.: 50,000
Length of Line: 10 miles	**Gauge:** Standard and Narrow gauge
	Web site: www.gwsr.com

GENERAL INFORMATION

Nearest Mainline Station: Cheltenham Spa or Ashchurch
Nearest Bus Station: Cheltenham
Car Parking: Parking available at Toddington, Winchcombe & Cheltenham Racecourse Stations
Coach Parking: Parking available as above
Souvenir Shop(s): Yes
Food & Drinks: Yes

SPECIAL INFORMATION

The North Gloucestershire narrow gauge railway also runs from Toddington Station. Gotherington Halt is now open with access by foot only.

OPERATING INFORMATION

Opening Times: Weekends and Bank Holidays from March to December. Also daily during School Holidays. 10.00am to 5.00pm
Steam Working: Most operating days
Prices: Adult Return £9.50
Child Return £6.00
Senior Citizen Return £8.00
Family Return £26.00 (2 Adult + 3 Child)
Under 5's free of charge

Detailed Directions by Car:
Toddington is 11 miles north east of Cheltenham, 5 miles south of Broadway just off the B4632 (old A46). Exit the M5 at Junction 9 towards Stow-on-the-Wold for the B4632. The Railway is clearly visible from the B4632.

GREAT CENTRAL RAILWAY

Address: Great Central Station, Great Central Road, Loughborough, Leicestershire LE11 1RW **Telephone Nº**: (01509) 230726 **Year Formed**: 1969 **Location of Line**: From Loughborough to Leicester	**Length of Line**: 8 miles **Nº of Steam Locos**: 10 **Nº of Other Locos**: 11 **Nº of Members**: 5,000 **Annual Membership Fee**: £25.00 **Approx Nº of Visitors P.A.**: 150,000 **Gauge**: Standard

GENERAL INFORMATION

Nearest Mainline Station: Loughborough (1 mile)
Nearest Bus Station: Loughborough (½ mile)
Car Parking: Street parking outside the Station
Coach Parking: Car parks at Quorn & Woodhouse, Rothley and Leicester North
Souvenir Shop(s): Yes
Food & Drinks: Yes – Buffet or Restaurant cars are usually available for snacks or other meals

Web site: www.gcrailway.co.uk

SPECIAL INFORMATION

The aim of the GCR is to recreate the experience of British main line railway operation during the best years of steam locomotives.

OPERATING INFORMATION

Opening Times: Open daily throughout the year.
Steam Working: Weekends and Bank Holidays throughout the year. Also selected weekdays in June, July and August.
Prices: Adult Day ticket £12.00
Child/Senior Citizen Day ticket £8.00
Family Day Ticket £30 (2 adults + 4 children)

Detailed Directions by Car:
Great Central Road is on the South East side of Loughborough and is clearly signposted from the A6 Leicester Road and A60 Nottingham Road.

GWILI RAILWAY

Address: Bronwydd Arms Station, Bronwydd Arms, Carmarthen   SA33 6HT
Telephone Nº: (01267) 230666
Year Formed: 1975
Location of Line: Near Carmarthen, South Wales
Length of Line: 2½ miles

Nº of Steam Locos: 5
Nº of Other Locos: 6
Nº of Members: 900 shareholders, 450 Society members
Annual Membership Fee: £10.00
Approx Nº of Visitors P.A.: 24,000
Gauge: Standard
Web site: www.gwili-railway.co.uk

GENERAL INFORMATION

Nearest Mainline Station: Carmarthen (3 miles)
Nearest Bus Station: Carmarthen (3 miles)
Car Parking: Free parking at Bronwydd Arms except for a few special occasions
Coach Parking: Free parking at Bronwydd Arms (but by arrangement only)
Souvenir Shop(s): Yes
Food & Drinks: Yes

SPECIAL INFORMATION

Gwili Railway was the first Standard Gauge preserved railway in Wales. There is a riverside picnic area and Miniature railway at Llwyfan Cerrig Station.

OPERATING INFORMATION

Opening Times: Daily from 23rd July to 31st August. Open over Easter, on Sundays in May, June, July & September and Wednesdays in June & July. Also open during school half-terms and dates in December. Please phone for further details.
Steam Working: Most advertised trains are steam hauled. Trains run from 11.15am to 4.30pm.
Prices: Adult   £5.50
    Child   £3.00
    Family £15.00 (2 adults + up to 2 children)
    Senior Citizens   £4.50

Detailed Directions by Car:
The Railway is three miles North of Carmarthen – signposted off the A484 Carmarthen to Cardigan Road.

ISLE OF WIGHT STEAM RAILWAY

Address: The Railway Station, Haven Street, Ryde, Isle of Wight   PO33 4DS
Telephone Nº: (01983) 882204
Year Formed: 1971 (re-opened)
Location: Smallbrook Junction to Wootton
Length of Line: 5 miles
Nº of Steam Locos: 7

Nº of Other Locos: 3
Nº of Members: 1,300
Annual Membership Fee: £15.00
Approx Nº of Visitors P.A.: 100,000
Gauge: Standard
Talking Timetable: (01983) 884343
Web site: www.iwsteamrailway.co.uk

GENERAL INFORMATION

Nearest Mainline Station: Smallbrook Junction (direct interchange)
Nearest Bus: From Ryde & Newport direct
Car Parking: Free parking at Havenstreet & Wootton Stations
Coach Parking: Free at Havenstreet Station
Souvenir Shop(s): Yes – at Havenstreet Station
Food & Drinks: Yes – at Havenstreet Station

SPECIAL INFORMATION

The IWSR uses mostly Victorian & Edwardian locomotives and carriages to recreate the atmosphere of an Isle of Wight branch line railway.

OPERATING INFORMATION

Opening Times: Selected days between March and October and daily from late May to mid-September
Steam Working: 10.30am to 4.00pm (depending on the Station)
Prices: Adult Return £8.50
                    Child Return £4.50
                    Family Return £22.00
                         (2 adults + 2 children)

Detailed Directions by Car:
To reach the Isle of Wight head for the Ferry ports at Lymington, Southampton or Portsmouth. From all parts of the Isle of Wight, head for Ryde and follow the brown tourist signs.

KEIGHLEY & WORTH VALLEY RAILWAY

Address: The Station, Haworth, Keighley, West Yorkshire BD22 8NJ **Telephone Nº:** (01535) 645214 (enquiries); (01535) 647777 (24 hour timetable) **Year Formed:** 1962 (Line re-opened 1968) **Location of Line:** From Keighley southwards through Haworth to Oxenhope **Length of Line:** 4¾ miles	**Nº of Steam Locos:** 30 **Nº of Other Locos:** 10 **Members:** 4,500 (350 working members) **Annual Membership Fee:** Adult £15.00; Adult life membership £300.00 **Approx Nº of Visitors P.A.:** 150,000 **Gauge:** Standard **Web Site:** www.kwvr.co.uk

GENERAL INFORMATION

Nearest Mainline Station: Keighley (adjacent)
Nearest Bus Station: Keighley (5 minutes walk)
Car Parking: Parking at Keighley, Ingrow, Haworth (charged) and Oxenhope
Coach Parking: At Ingrow & Oxenhope (phone in advance)
Souvenir Shop(s): Yes – at Keighley, Haworth & Oxenhope
Food & Drinks: Yes – at Keighley & Oxenhope when trains run.

OPERATING INFORMATION

Opening Times: Weekends & Bank Holidays throughout the year. Daily from 1st July to 3rd September. Also open during Easter, Whit, October School holidays and 26th December to 1st January.
Steam Working: Early trains are Diesel; Steam runs from mid-morning on all operating days (except 4 weekends prior to Christmas).
Prices: Adult Return £8.00; £12.00 day rover
Child Return £4.00; £6.00 day rover
Family Return £20.00 (2 adults, 3 children)
Family Day Rover £25.00

Detailed Directions by Car:
Exit the M62 at Junction 26 and take the M606 to its' end. Follow the ring-road signs around Bradford to Shipley. Take the A650 through Bingley to Keighley and follow the brown tourist signs to the railway. Alternatively, take the A6033 from Hebden Bridge to Oxenhope and follow the brown signs to Oxenhope or Haworth Stations.

KENT & EAST SUSSEX RAILWAY

Address: Tenterden Town Station, Tenterden, Kent TN30 6HE
Telephone Nº: 087 060 060 74
Year Formed: 1973
Location of Line: Tenterden, Kent to Bodiam, East Sussex
Length of Line: 10½ miles

Nº of Steam Locos: 12
Nº of Other Locos: 6
Nº of Members: 3,000
Annual Membership Fee: £21.50
Approx Nº of Visitors P.A.: 110,000
Gauge: Standard
Web site: www.kesr.org.uk

GENERAL INFORMATION

Nearest Mainline Station: Headcorn (8 miles)
Nearest Bus Station: Tenterden
Car Parking: Free parking available at Tenderden Town and Northiam Stations
Coach Parking: Tenderden & Northiam
Souvenir Shop(s): Yes
Food & Drinks: Yes

SPECIAL INFORMATION

Built as Britain's first light railway, the K&ESR opened in 1900 and was epitomised by sharp curved and steep gradients and to this day retains a charm and atmosphere all of its own.

OPERATING INFORMATION

Opening Times: From March to October and in December. The return journey time is 1 hour 55 minutes. Please phone the 24 hour talking-timetable for precise operating information: (01580) 762943
Steam Working: Every operational day
Prices: Adult Ticket – £10.50
Child Ticket – £5.50
Family Ticket – £27.00
Note: The prices shown above are for Day Rover tickets which allow unlimited travel on the day of purchase.

Detailed Directions by Car:
From London and Kent Coast: Travel to Ashford (M20) then take the A28 to Tenterden; From Sussex Coast: Take A28 from Hastings to Northiam.

LAKESIDE & HAVERTHWAITE RAILWAY

Address: Haverthwaite Station, near Ulverston, Cumbria   LA12 8AL
Telephone Nº: (015395) 31594
Year Formed: 1973
Location of Line: Haverthwaite to Lakeside
Length of Line: 3½ miles

Nº of Steam Locos: 8
Nº of Other Locos: 6
Nº of Members: 250
Annual Membership Fee: £10.00 Adult, £5.00 Juniors
Approx Nº of Visitors P.A.: 170,000
Gauge: Standard

GENERAL INFORMATION

Nearest Mainline Station: Ulverston (7 miles)
Nearest Bus Station: Haverthwaite (100 yards)
Car Parking: Plenty of spaces – £1.50 charge
Coach Parking: Free parking at site
Souvenir Shop(s): Yes
Food & Drinks: Yes

SPECIAL INFORMATION

Connections are available at Lakeside for Windermere Lake Cruises to Bowness & Ambleside. Through tickets are available.

OPERATING INFORMATION

Opening Times: Daily from 1st April to 29th October inclusive. Santa Specials run on 2nd, 3rd, 9th, 10th, 16th and 17th of December.
Steam Working: Daily from morning to late afternoon.
Prices: Adult Return £4.90   Single £2.95
             Child Return £2.45   Single £2.00
             Family Ticket £13.50

Web site: www.lakesiderailway.co.uk

Detailed Directions by Car:
From All Parts: Exit the M6 at Junction 36 and follow the brown tourist signs.

THE LAVENDER LINE

Address: Isfield Station, Isfield, near Uckfield, East Sussex TN22 5XB	**Nº of Steam Locos**: 2
Telephone Nº: (01825) 750515	**Nº of Other Locos**: 1 + DEMU
Year Formed: 1992	**Nº of Members**: Approximately 400
Location of Line: East Sussex between Lewes and Uckfield	**Annual Membership Fee**: £15.00
Length of Line: 1 mile	**Approx Nº of Visitors P.A.**: 12,500
	Gauge: Standard
	Web site: www.lavender-line.co.uk

GENERAL INFORMATION

Nearest Mainline Station: Uckfield (3 miles)
Nearest Bus Station: Uckfield (3 miles)
Car Parking: Free parking at site
Coach Parking: Can cater for coach parties – please contact the Railway.
Souvenir Shop: Yes
Food & Drinks: Yes – Cinders Buffet

SPECIAL INFORMATION

Isfield Station has been restored as a Southern Railway country station complete with the original L.B.S.C.R. signalbox.

OPERATING INFORMATION

Opening Times: Sundays throughout the year. Saturdays and Sundays in June, July and August plus Wednesdays in July and August. Also open on Bank Holidays and in December for Santa Specials.
Steam Working: Please phone for details.
Prices: Adult £6.00
        Child £4.00
        Senior Citizen £5.00
        Family (2 adults + 3 children) £18.00
All tickets offer unlimited rides on the day of issue and prices may vary on special event days.

Detailed Directions by Car::
From All Parts: Isfield is just off the A26 midway between Lewes and Uckfield.

LINCOLNSHIRE WOLDS RAILWAY

Address: The Railway Station, Ludborough, Lincolnshire DN36 5SQ
Telephone Nº: (01507) 363881
Year Formed: 1979
Location of Line: Ludborough – off the A16(T) between Grimsby and Louth
Length of Line: ¾ mile

Nº of Steam Locos: 3   **Other Locos**: 7
Nº of Members of the Supporting Society (GLRPS): 400+
Annual Membership Fee: £14.00 Family, £7.00 Adult, £4.50 Senior Citizen or Child
Approx Nº of Visitors P.A.: 5,000
Gauge: Standard

GENERAL INFORMATION

Nearest Mainline Station: Grimsby (8 miles)
Nearest Bus Stop: Ludborough (½ mile)
Car Parking: 100 spaces for cars at the Station
Coach Parking: Space for 1 coach only
Souvenir Shop(s): Yes
Food & Drinks: Yes

SPECIAL INFORMATION

The buildings and facilities at Ludborough have been completed and short steam trips commenced in 1998. Plans to extend the line to North Thoresby (1 mile) are well underway.

OPERATING INFORMATION

Opening Times: Certain Sundays from January to December. Also Santa Specials in December. Advance bookings are essential.
Steam Working: Contact the Railway for details.
Prices: Adults £3.50
         Senior Citizens/Children £2.00
         Family £8.00 (2 adults + 4 children)
Different fares may apply at Special Events. Prices include unlimited rides throughout the day.

Web site: www.lincolnshirewoldsrailway.co.uk

Detailed Directions by Car:
The Railway is situated near Ludborough, ½ mile off the A16(T) Louth to Grimsby road. Follow signs to Fulstow to reach the station (approximately ½ mile). Do not turn into Ludborough but stay on the bypass.

LLANGOLLEN RAILWAY

Address: The Station, Abbey Road, Llangollen, Denbighshire LL20 8SN **Telephone Nº:** (01978) 860979 **Year Formed:** 1975 **Location of Line:** Valley of the River Dee from Llangollen to Carrog **Length of Line:** 7½ miles	**Nº of Steam Locos:** 14 **Nº of Other Locos:** 13 **Nº of Members:** 1,300 **Annual Membership Fee:** Adult £13.00; Family £20.00; Junior (under-16) £8.00 **Approx Nº of Visitors P.A.:** 90,000 **Gauge:** Standard

GENERAL INFORMATION

Nearest Mainline Station: Ruabon (6 miles)
Nearest Bus Station: Wrexham (12 miles)
Car Parking: Public car park at Lower Dee Mill off A539 Ruabon road.
Coach Parking: Market Street car park in town centre
Souvenir Shop(s): Yes – at Llangollen Station
Food & Drinks: Yes – at Llangollen, Berwyn, Glyndyfrdwy and Carrog Stations.

SPECIAL INFORMATION

The route originally formed part of the line from Ruabon to Barmouth Junction, closed in 1964. The railway has been rebuilt by volunteers since 1975, reopening to Carrog in 1996.
The ultimate aim is to reopen to Corwen (10 miles).

OPERATING INFORMATION

Opening Times: Services run daily from 8th April to 5th November. Also on weekends in December, other Santa Specials near Christmas and a number of other dates throughout the year.
Steam Working: Phone the Talking timetable number for further details: (01978) 860951
Prices: Adult Return £8.00 (Llangollen to Carrog)
Child Return £4.00
Family £18.00 (2 adults + 2 children)
Senior Citizens £6.00
Note: Shorter journeys are cheaper.

Web Site: www.llangollen-railway.co.uk

Detailed Directions by Car:
From South & West: Go via the A5 to Llangollen. At the traffic lights turn into Castle Street to the River bridge; From North & East: Take the A483 to A539 junction and then via Trefor to Llangollen River bridge. The Station is adjacent to the River Dee.

MANGAPPS RAILWAY MUSEUM

Address: Southminster Road, Burnham-on-Crouch, Essex CM0 8QQ **Telephone Nº:** (01621) 784898 **Year Formed:** 1989 **Location of Line:** Mangapps Farm **Length of Line:** ¾ mile	**Nº of Steam Locos:** 6 **Nº of Other Locos:** 7 **Nº of Members:** – **Annual Membership Fee:** – **Approx Nº of Visitors P.A.:** 20,000 **Gauge:** Standard

GENERAL INFORMATION

Nearest Mainline Station: Burnham-on-Crouch (1 mile)
Nearest Bus Station: –
Car Parking: Ample free parking at site
Coach Parking: Ample free parking at site
Souvenir Shop(s): Yes
Food & Drinks: Yes – drinks and snacks only

SPECIAL INFORMATION

The Railway endeavours to recreate the atmosphere of an East Anglian light railway. It also includes an extensive museum with an emphasis on East Anglian items and signalling.

Web Site: www.mangapps.co.uk

OPERATING INFORMATION

Opening Times: Closed during January, then open every weekend and bank holiday (except over Christmas). Open every day during the August School Holidays and for a number of other special events throughout the year. Santa Specials run during weekends in December. Please contact the railway for further details.
Steam Working: Bank Holiday Sundays and Mondays only. Diesel at other times.
Prices: Adult – Steam £6.00;   Diesel £5.00
 Child – Steam £3.00;   Diesel £2.50
 Senior Citizen – Steam £5.00; Diesel £4.00
Note: Prices for special events may differ.

Detailed Directions by Car:
From South & West: From M25 take either the A12 or A127 and then the A130 to Rettendon Turnpike and then follow signs to Burnham; From North: From A12 take A414 to Oak Corner then follow signs to Burnham.

THE MIDDLETON RAILWAY

Address: The Station, Moor Road, Hunslet, Leeds LS10 2JQ
Telephone Nº: (0113) 271-0320
Year Formed: 1960
Location of Line: Moor Road to Middleton Park
Length of Line: 1½ miles

Nº of Steam Locos: 15
Nº of Other Locos: 12
Annual Membership Fee: Adults £9.50
Approx Nº of Visitors P.A.: 20,000
Gauge: Standard
Web Site: www.middletonrailway.org.uk

GENERAL INFORMATION

Nearest Mainline Station: Leeds City (1 mile)
Nearest Bus Station: Leeds (1½ miles)
Car Parking: Free parking at site
Coach Parking: Free parking at site
Souvenir Shop(s): Yes
Food & Drinks: Yes

SPECIAL INFORMATION

The Middleton Railway is the world's oldest working railway, founded in 1758. Passenger services run from the station into Middleton Park. A large collection of preserved industrial steam and diesel engines are displayed, many of them more than 100 years old.

OPERATING INFORMATION

Opening Times: The Railway intends to re-open on Saturday 15th April 2006 and will then open every Saturday until 28th October from 1.00pm to 4.20pm. It will also be open every Sunday and Bank Holiday from 16th April to 26th November from 11.00am to 4.20pm. Santa Specials will run on weekends in December. Should the engineering work over run, the accuracy of the timetable above cannot be guaranteed. Contact the railway for the latest information.
Steam Working: Most operating Sundays – please contact the railway for details.
Prices: Adult £4.50
        Child £2.50
        Family £12.00
            (2 adults + 3 children)
Tickets provide for unlimited travel on the day of issue.
Please send a SAE for the timetable and details of special events or check the web site.

Detailed Directions by Car:
From the South: Take the M621 Northbound and exit at Junction 5. Turn right at the top of the slip road and take the 3rd exit at the roundabout. The Railway is 50 yards on the right; From the West: Take the M621 Southbound and exit at Junction 4. Go straight on at the end of the slip road then take the 2nd exit at the roundabout.

MID-HANTS RAILWAY (WATERCRESS LINE)

Address: The Railway Station, Alresford, Hampshire SO24 9JG
Telephone Nº: (01962) 733810 General enquiries; (01962) 734866 Timetable
Year Formed: 1977
Location of Line: Alresford to Alton
Length of Line: 10 miles

Nº of Steam Locos: 16
Nº of Other Locos: 8
Nº of Members: 4,500
Annual Membership Fee: Adult £20.00
Approx Nº of Visitors P.A.: 130,000
Gauge: Standard
Web Site: www.watercressline.co.uk

GENERAL INFO

Nearest Mainline Station: Alton (adjacent) or Winchester (7 miles)
Nearest Bus Station: Winchester or Alton
Car Parking: Pay and display at Alton and Alresford Stations (Alresford free on Sundays & Bank Holidays)
Coach Parking: By arrangement at Alresford Station
Souvenir Shop(s): At Alresford, Ropley & Alton
Food & Drinks: Yes – Buffet on most trains. 'West Country' buffet at Alresford

SPECIAL INFO

The railway runs through four fully restored stations and has a Loco yard and picnic area at Ropley.

OPERATING INFO

Opening Times: Weekends and Bank Holidays from January to October. Weekdays from May to September and during School Holidays. Santa Specials run at weekends and on other dates in December.
Steam Working: All operating days although a Steam/DMU combination is sometimes in service.
Prices: Adult £10.00
Child (age 3 to 16) £5.00
Senior Citizens £9.00
Family £25.00
(2 adults + 2 children)
A discount is available for pre-booked parties of 15 or more people. Write or call for a booking form.

Detailed Directions by Car:
From the East: Take the M25 then A3 and A31 to Alton; From the West: Exit the M3 at Junction 9 and take the A31 to Alresford Station.

MID-NORFOLK RAILWAY

Address: The Railway Station, Station Road, East Dereham NR19 1DF **Telephone Nº:** (01362) 690633 or 851723 **Year Formed:** 1995 **Location:** East Dereham to Wymondham **Length of Line:** 11 miles **Web site:** www.mnr.org.uk	**Nº of Steam Locos:** No Steam as yet but the Trust hopes to have it shortly. **Nº of Other Locos:** 5 **Nº of Members:** 1,000 **Annual Membership Fee:** £15.00 **Approx Nº of Visitors P.A.:** 10,000 **Gauge:** Standard

GENERAL INFORMATION

Nearest Mainline Station: Wymondham (1 mile)
Nearest Bus Station: Wymondham or East Dereham – each ½ mile away
Car Parking: Available at Dereham Station
Coach Parking: Available at Dereham Station
Souvenir Shop(s): Yes – at Dereham Station
Food & Drinks: Yes – at Dereham Station

SPECIAL INFORMATION

The Mid-Norfolk Railway aims to preserve part of the former Great Eastern Railway from Wymondham to Wells-next-the-Sea. The section from Wymondham to Dereham was opened to passenger and freight traffic in May 1999 and clearance work is now complete on the East Dereham to North Elmham section.

OPERATING INFORMATION

Opening Times: Every Sunday and Bank Holiday from 5th March to 19th November. Also open on Saturdays from 18th March to 28th October, Wednesdays from 10th May to 25th October and Thursdays from 27th July to 7th September.
Steam Working: None at present but planned in the future.
Prices: Adult Return £6.00 (Diesel)
                Child Return £3.00 (Diesel)

Detailed Directions by Car:
From All Parts: From the A47 bypass, turn into East Dereham and follow the signs for the Town Centre. Turn right at the BP Garage – look out for the brown tourist signs – you will see the Station on your right.

MID-SUFFOLK LIGHT RAILWAY MUSEUM

Address: Brockford Station, Wetheringsett, Suffolk IP14 5PW **Telephone Nº**: (01449) 766899 **Year Formed**: 1990 **Location of Line**: Wetheringsett, Suffolk **Length of Line**: ¼ mile	**Nº of Steam Locos**: 2 (1 operational) **Nº of Other Locos**: 1 **Nº of Members**: 300 **Annual Membership Fee**: £10.00 **Approx Nº of Visitors P.A.**: 1,750 **Gauge**: Standard **Web site**: www.mslr.org.uk

GENERAL INFORMATION

Nearest Mainline Station: Stowmarket
Nearest Bus Station: Ipswich
Car Parking: Available on site
Coach Parking: Available on site
Souvenir Shop(s): Yes
Food & Drinks: Yes

SPECIAL INFORMATION

The Mid-Suffolk Light Railway served the heart of the county for 50 years, despite being bankrupt before the first train ran. In a beautiful rural setting, the Museum seeks to preserve the memory of a unique branch line.

OPERATING INFORMATION

Opening Times: Sundays and Bank Holiday Mondays from Easter to the end of September – 11.00am to 5.00pm. Also on Wednesdays in August from 1.00pm to 5.00pm and Special events at other times.
Steam Working: 16th, 17th & 30th April; 1st, 28th & 29th May; 18th June; 2nd July; 6th, 13th, 20th, 27th & 28th August; 10th September; 10th & 17th December. Possibly other dates – contact the railway or check the web site for details.
Prices: Adult £5.00
              Child £2.50
Tickets allow unlimited travel on the day of issue.

Detailed Directions by Car:
The Museum is situated 14 miles north of Ipswich and 28 miles south of Norwich, just off the A140. Look for Mendlesham TV mast and then follow the brown tourist signs from the A140.

MIDLAND RAILWAY – BUTTERLEY

Address: Butterley Station, Ripley, Derbyshire DE5 3QZ
Telephone Nº: (01773) 747674
Year Formed: 1969
Location of Line: Butterley, near Ripley
Length of Line: Standard gauge 3½ miles, Narrow gauge 0.8 mile

Nº of Steam Locos: 25
Nº of Other Locos: 53
Nº of Members: 2,000
Annual Membership Fee: £14.00
Approx Nº of Visitors P.A.: 130,000
Gauge: Standard, various Narrow gauges and miniature

GENERAL INFORMATION

Nearest Mainline Station: Alfreton (6 miles)
Nearest Bus Station: Bus stop outside Butterley Station.
Car Parking: Free parking at site – ample space
Coach Parking: Free parking at site
Souvenir Shop(s): Yes – at Butterley and Swanwick
Food & Drinks: Yes – both sites + bar on train

SPECIAL INFORMATION

The Centre is a unique project with a huge Museum development together with narrow gauge, miniature & model railways as well as a country park and farm park. Includes an Award-winning Victorian Railwayman's church and Princess Royal Class Locomotive Trust Depot.

OPERATING INFORMATION

Opening Times: The centre is open daily – trains do not run every day it is open however.
Steam Working: Weekends and bank holidays throughout the year and most days in the school holidays. Phone for further details. 'Day Out With Thomas' 2006 events: 4th, 5th, 11th & 12th March; 27th May to 4th June; 29th July to 6th August and 14th & 15th October.
Prices: Adult £8.95   Senior Citizens £7.95
   Children £4.50
Note: Supplements are charged for some special events

Detailed Directions by Car:
From All Parts: From the M1 exit at Junction 28 and take the A38 towards Derby. The Centre is signposted at the junction with the B6179.

NENE VALLEY RAILWAY

Address: Wansford Station, Stibbington, Peterborough   PE8 6LR
Telephone Nº: (01780) 784444 enquiries; (01780) 784404 talking timetable
Year Formed: 1977
Location: Off A1 to west of Peterborough
Length of Line: 7½ miles

Nº of Steam Locos: 17
Nº of Other Locos: 11
Nº of Members: 1,300
Annual Membership Fee: Adult £14.00; Child £8.00; Joint £21.50; OAP £8.00
Approx Nº of Visitors P.A.: 65,000
Gauge: Standard

GENERAL INFORMATION

Nearest Mainline Station: Peterborough (¾ mile)
Nearest Bus Station: Peterborough (Queensgate – ¾ mile)
Car Parking: Free parking at Wansford & Orton Mere
Coach Parking: Free coach parking at Wansford
Souvenir Shop(s): Yes
Food & Drinks: Yes

SPECIAL INFORMATION

The railway is truly international in flavour with British and Continental locomotives and rolling stock.

Web site: www.nvr.org.uk

OPERATING INFORMATION

Opening Times: Sundays from January to the end of October. Saturdays from Easter to end of October. Mid-week on various dates from May to the end of August and also at various other times. Contact the Railway for complete details. Open 9.00am to 4.30pm.
Steam Working: Most services are steam hauled apart from on diesel days and times of high fire risk.
Prices: Adult £10.50 (Special events £13.00) Child £5.50 (age 3-15) (Special events £6.50) Family £26.00 (2 adult + 3 child) (Special £32.00) Senior Citizens/Disabled £8.00 (Special £10.00)

Detailed Directions by Car:
The railway is situated off the southbound carriageway of the A1 between the A47 and A605 junctions – west of Peterborough and south of Stamford.

NORTHAMPTON & LAMPORT RAILWAY

Address: Pitsford & Bramford Station, Pitsford Road, Chapel Brampton, Northampton NN6 8BA **Telephone Nº**: (01604) 820327 (infoline) **Year Formed**: 1983 (became operational in November 1995) **Web site**: www.nlr.org.uk	**Length of Line**: 1¼ miles at present **Nº of Steam Locos**: 6 **Nº of Other Locos**: 10 **Nº of Members**: 600 **Annual Membership Fee**: £10.00 **Approx Nº of Visitors P.A.**: 20,000 **Gauge**: Standard

GENERAL INFORMATION

Nearest Mainline Station: Northampton (5 miles)
Nearest Bus Station: Northampton (5 miles)
Car Parking: Free parking at site
Coach Parking: Free parking at site
Souvenir Shop(s): Yes
Food & Drinks: Yes

SPECIAL INFORMATION

A developing railway – this became operational again on 18th November 1995.

OPERATING INFORMATION

Opening Times: Sundays and Bank holidays from March to October. Santa Specials in December. Open 10.30am to 5.00pm.
Steam Working: Generally between April and September and also in December.
Prices: Adult £3.60
         Child £2.60
         Family £10.00 (2 adults + 2 children)
         Senior Citizen £2.60
Fares may vary on Special Event days.

Detailed Directions by Car:
The station is situated along the Pitsford road at Chapel Brampton, approximately 5 miles north of Northampton. Heading north out of town, it is signposted to the right on the A5199 (A50) Welford Road at Chapel Brampton crossroads or on the left on the A508 Market Harborough road at the Pitsford turn.

NORTH NORFOLK RAILWAY

Address: Sheringham Station, Sheringham, Norfolk NR26 8RA	**Nº of Steam Locos**: 7
Telephone Nº: (01263) 820800	**Nº of Other Locos**: 4
Year Formed: 1975	**Nº of Members**: 1,600
Location of Line: Sheringham to Holt via Weybourne	**Annual Membership Fee**: £14.00
	Approx Nº of Visitors P.A.: 130,000
Length of Line: 5½ miles	**Gauge**: Standard
	Web site: www.nnr.co.uk

GENERAL INFORMATION

Nearest Mainline Station: Sheringham (200 yards)
Nearest Bus Station: Outside the Station
Car Parking: Adjacent to all three stations
Coach Parking: Adjacent to all three stations
Souvenir Shop(s): At Sheringham Station
Food & Drinks: Yes – main catering facilities at Sheringham Station. Light refreshments elsewhere.

SPECIAL INFORMATION

William Marriott Railway Museum is due to open at Holt Station in Summer 2006. The line was once part of the Midland & Great Northern Joint Railway.

OPERATING INFORMATION

Opening Times: Most days from mid-March to the end of October plus Santa Specials in December.
Special Events: Steam Galas on 6th to 8th October + 31st December to 2nd January; Beer Festival 14th to 16th July; 1940s Weekend 16th & 17th September; Day out with Thomas 21st to 23rd October.
Steam Working: 10.30am to 4.30pm
Prices: Adult £9.00
Child £5.50   (Under 4's free of charge)
Family £27.00 (includes free brochure)
Senior Citizens £8.00
All the above prices are all-day Steaming-day tickets.

Detailed Directions by Car:
The railway is situated on the A149 Cromer to Sheringham road. All 3 stations are signposted from this road.

NORTH TYNESIDE STEAM RAILWAY

Address: Stephenson Railway Museum, Middle Engine Lane, North Shields, NE29 8DX
Telephone Nº: (0191) 200-7146
Year Formed: 1986
Location: Stephenson Railway Museum
Length of Line: 1½ miles

Nº of Steam Locos: 5
Nº of Other Locos: 3
Nº of Members: None
Annual Membership Fee: £8.00
Approx Nº of Visitors P.A.: 30,000
Gauge: Standard
Web site: www.ntsra.org.uk

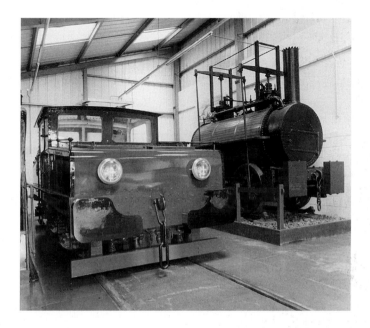

GENERAL INFORMATION

Nearest Mainline Station: Newcastle Central (5 miles)
Nearest Bus Station: North Shields
Car Parking: Free parking available on site
Coach Parking: Free parking available on site
Souvenir Shop(s): No
Food & Drinks: On major event days only

SPECIAL INFORMATION

A programme of events and activities is available from the Museum on request.

OPERATING INFORMATION

Opening Times: Weekends and daily during School Holidays from May to October, 11.00am to 4.00pm
Steam Working: Sundays and Bank Holiday Mondays from June to September.
Prices: Adult Return £2.00
Child Return £1.00
Family Return £5.00

Detailed Directions by Car:
The Railway is adjacent to the Silverlink Retail Park approximately ½ mile from the junction between the A19 and A1058. From the A19/A1058 junction look for the signs for 'Silverlink' before following the Brown tourist signs to the Stephenson Railway Museum.

NORTH YORKSHIRE MOORS RAILWAY

Address: Pickering Station, Pickering, North Yorkshire YO18 7AJ **Telephone N°:** (01751) 472508 (enquiries) **Web site:** www.northyorkshiremoorsrailway.com **Year Formed:** 1967 **Location of Line:** Pickering to Grosmont via stations at Levisham and Goathland	**Length of Line:** 18 miles **N° of Steam Locos:** 20 **N° of Other Locos:** 12 **N° of Members:** 8,000 **Annual Membership Fee:** Adult £16.00; Over 60's £12.00 **Approx N° of Visitors P.A.:** 300,000 **Gauge:** Standard

GENERAL INFORMATION

Nearest Mainline Station: Grosmont (adjacent to the NYMR station)
Nearest Bus Station: Pickering (½ mile)
Car Parking: Available at each station
Coach Parking: Available at Pickering & Grosmont
Souvenir Shop(s): Yes – at Pickering, Goathland, and Grosmont Stations plus Grosmont MPD
Food & Drinks: Pickering, Grosmont & Goathland

SPECIAL INFORMATION

The NYMR runs through the spectacular North Yorkshire Moors National Park and is the most popular in the country. As seen in 'Heartbeat' and the first Harry Potter film.

OPERATING INFORMATION

Opening Times: Open daily from 1st April to 29th October plus Santa Specials in December.
Steam Working: Usually daily – please phone the Railway for timetable information
Prices: Adult £14.00 (all-day travel)
Child £7.00 (all-day travel)
Family Tickets start at £29.00 for 2 adults & 1 child –
£30.00 for 2 adults and 2 children
£31.00 for 2 adults and 3 children
£32.00 for 2 adults and 4 children

Detailed Directions by Car:
From the South: Follow the A64 past York to the Malton bypass then take the A169 to Pickering; From the North: Take A171 towards Whitby then follow the minor road through Egton to Grosmont.

NOTTINGHAM TRANSPORT HERITAGE CENTRE

Address: Nottingham Transport Heritage
Centre, Mere Way, Ruddington,
Nottingham   NG11 6NX
Telephone Nº: (0115) 940-5705
Fax Nº: (0115) 940-5905
Year Formed: 1990 (Opened in 1994)
Location of Line: Ruddington to

Loughborough Junction
Length of Line: 9 miles
Nº of Steam Locos: 6
Nº of Other Locos: 7
Nº of Members: 850
Annual Membership Fee: £12.00
Approx Nº of Visitors P.A.: 15,000

GENERAL INFORMATION

Nearest Mainline Station: Nottingham (5 miles)
Nearest Bus Station: Bus service from Nottingham
to the Centre
Car Parking: Free parking at site
Coach Parking: Free parking at site
Souvenir Shop(s): Yes
Food & Drinks: Yes

SPECIAL INFORMATION

The Heritage Centre covers an area of over eleven
acres and is set within the Rushcliffe Country Park
in Ruddington. Trains run to Rushcliffe Halt.

OPERATING INFORMATION

Opening Times: Sundays and Bank Holidays from
2nd April until the 8th October. Open 10.45am to
5.00pm. Also open for Santa Specials on December
weekends.
Steam Working: Steam service runs from 11.00am
Prices: Adult £6.00
             Child £3.00
             Senior Citizens £5.00
             Family £17.00 (2 adults + 3 children)

Web Site: www.nthc.co.uk

Detailed Directions by Car:
From All Parts: The centre is situated off the A60 Nottingham to Loughborough Road and is signposted just
south of the traffic lights at Ruddington.

PAIGNTON & DARTMOUTH STEAM RAILWAY

Address: Queen's Park Station, Torbay Road, Paignton TQ4 6AF	**N° of Steam Locos:** 6
	N° of Other Locos: 3
Telephone N°: (01803) 555872	**N° of Members:** –
Year Formed: 1973	**Annual Membership Fee:** –
Location of Line: Paignton to Kingswear	**Approx N° of Visitors P.A.:** 350,000
Length of Line: 7 miles	**Gauge:** Standard

GENERAL INFORMATION

Nearest Mainline Station: Paignton (adjacent)
Nearest Bus Station: Paignton (2 minutes walk)
Car Parking: Multi-storey or Mainline Station
Coach Parking: Multi-storey (3 minutes walk)
Souvenir Shop(s): Yes – at Paignton & Kingswear
Food & Drinks: Yes – at Paignton & Kinswear

SPECIAL INFORMATION

A passenger ferry is available from Kingswear Station across to Dartmouth. Combined excursions are also available including train and river trips.

Web site: www.paignton-steamrailway.co.uk

OPERATING INFORMATION

Opening Times: Open daily from June to September (inclusive). Also open days in April, May, October and December (phone for details).
Steam Working: Trains run throughout the day from 10.30am to 5.00pm
Prices: Adult Return £9.00
           Child Return £6.00
Family Return £28.00 (2 adults + 2 children)
Note: Cheaper fares are charged for shorter journeys

Detailed Directions by Car:
From All Parts: Take the M5 to Exeter and then the A380 to Paignton.

PALLOT STEAM, MOTOR & GENERAL MUSEUM

Address: Rue de Bechet, Trinity, Jersey, JE3 5BE
Telephone N°: (01534) 865307
Year Formed: 1990
Location of Line: Trinity, Jersey
Length of Line: A third of a mile

N° of Steam Locos: 4
N° of Other Locos: 2
N° of Members: None
Approx N° of Visitors P.A.: 12,000
Gauge: Standard and Narrow gauge
Web site: www.pallotmuseum.co.uk

GENERAL INFORMATION

Nearest Mainline Station: None
Nearest Bus Station: St. Helier
Car Parking: Available on site
Coach Parking: Available on site
Souvenir Shop(s): Yes
Food & Drinks: Snacks only

SPECIAL INFORMATION

The museum was founded by Lyndon (Don) Pallot who spent his early career as a trainee engineer with the old Jersey Railway.

OPERATING INFORMATION

Opening Times: Daily from 1st April to 31st October. Open from 10.00am to 5.00pm. Closed on Sundays.
Steam Working: Every Thursday and also on high-season Tuesdays.
Prices: Adult Museum Admission £4.50
Child Museum Admission £1.50
Senior Citizen Museum Admission £4.00
Adult Train Ride £1.50
Child Train Ride £1.00

Detailed Directions by Car:
The museum lies between the A8 and the A9 main roads (Bus Route 5 is easiest) and is signposted off both of these roads.

PEAK RAIL PLC

Address: Matlock Station, Matlock, Derbyshire DE4 3NA
Telephone Nº: (01629) 580381
Fax Nº: (01629) 760645
Year Formed: 1975
Location of Line: Matlock Riverside to Rowsley South

Length of Line: 4 miles
Nº of Steam Locos: 6 **Other Locos:** 20+
Nº of Members: 1,700
Annual Adult Membership Fee: £15.00
Approx Nº of Visitors P.A.: 40,000
Gauge: Standard
Web site: www.peakrail.co.uk

GENERAL INFO

Nearest Mainline Station: Matlock (500 yards)
Nearest Bus Station: Matlock
Car Parking: Paid car parking at Matlock Station, 200 spaces at Rowsley South Station, 20 spaces at Darley Dale Station
Coach Parking: Free parking at Rowsley South
Souvenir Shop(s): Yes
Food & Drinks: Yes

SPECIAL INFO

The Palatine Restaurant Car is available whilst travelling on the train and caters for Sunday Lunches, Teas and Party Bookings. Coach parties are welcomed when the railway is operating.

OPERATING INFO

Opening Times: Sundays from January to March and in November. Weekends during the rest of the year. Also Wednesdays and Thursdays in June and July, Tuesdays, Wednesdays and Thursdays in August and Wednesdays in September.
Steam Working: All services throughout the year.
Prices: Adult Return £6.00
Children – Under-3's Free
Children – Ages 3-5 £1.00
Children – Ages 6-15 £3.00
Senior Citizen Return £4.60
Family Ticket
(2 adults + 3 children) £17.00

Detailed Directions by Car:
Exit the M1 at Junctions 28, 29 or 30 and follow signs towards Matlock. From North and South take A6 direct to Matlock. From Stoke-on-Trent, take the A52 to Ashbourne, then the A5035 to Matlock. Upon reaching Matlock follow the brown tourist signs.

PLYM VALLEY RAILWAY

Address: Marsh Mills Station, Coypool Road, Plympton, Plymouth PL7 4NW	**Nº of Steam Locos**: 3
Telephone Nº: (01752) 330881	**Nº of Other Locos**: 3
Year Formed: 1980	**Nº of Members**: 200
Location of Line: Marsh Mills to World's End, Plympton	**Annual Membership Fee**: £10.00
	Approx Nº of Visitors P.A.: 5,000
Length of Line: ½ mile	**Gauge**: Standard
	Web site: www.plymrail.co.uk

GENERAL INFORMATION

Nearest Mainline Station: Plymouth (4 miles)
Nearest Bus Station: Plymouth (3 miles)
Car Parking: Available on site
Coach Parking: Available on site
Souvenir Shop(s): Yes
Food & Drinks: Light snacks available

SPECIAL INFORMATION

It is planned to extend the line to Plymbridge, a distance of 1¼ miles.

OPERATING INFORMATION

Opening Times: Most Sundays from 10.00am to 5.00pm. Not every open day has trains operating, however.
Steam Working: Second Sunday in every month from April to November. Also the fourth Sunday of the month from June to September. Trains run from 1.00pm to 4.00pm.
Prices: Adult Return £1.50
              Child Return 75p
Note: There is no charge to visit the station.

Detailed Directions by Car:
Leave the A38 at the Marsh Mills turn-off and take the B3416 towards Plympton. Turn left into Coypool Road just after the McDonalds restaurant. From Plymouth City Centre, take the A374 to Marsh Mills, then as above.

PONTYPOOL & BLAENAVON RAILWAY

Address: 13a Broad Street, Blaenavon, Torfaen NP4 9ND
e-mail: pbrsec@aol.com
Telephone No: (01495) 792263 or 760242
Year Formed: 1980 (Opened 1983)
Location of Line: Just off the B4248 between Blaenavon and Brynmawr
Length of Line: ¾ mile

No of Steam Locos: 9
No of Other Locos: 7 + 3 DMUs
No of Members: 200
Annual Membership Fee: £10.00
Approx No of Visitors P.A.: 4,500
Gauge: Standard
Web site: www.pontypool-and-blaenavon.co.uk

GENERAL INFORMATION

Nearest Mainline Station: Abergavenny (5 miles)
Nearest Bus Station: Blaenavon Town (1½ miles) – regular bus service within ¼ mile (except Sundays)
Car Parking: Free parking for 50 cars on site
Coach Parking: Available on site
Souvenir Shop(s): Yes – on the train (usually) and also a shop at 13 Broad Street, Blaenavon
Food & Drinks: Light refreshments on the train

SPECIAL INFORMATION

The railway operates over very steep gradients, is run entirely by volunteers and is the highest standard gauge preserved railway in England and Wales.

OPERATING INFORMATION

Opening Times: Every Sunday and Bank Holiday Monday from Easter to the end of September. Also many Saturdays throughout the year. Santa Specials and other Special events also run. Please phone the Railway for details or check the web site.
Steam Working: No steaming at present – services are worked by Diesel locos or DMU.
Prices: Adult £2.40   (unlimited travel
                Child £1.20   on the day of issue
                Family £6.00   with ordinary returns)
Fares and conditions can vary for Special Events.

Detailed Directions by Car:
From All Parts: The railway is situated just off the B4248 between Blaenavon and Brynmawr and is well signposted as you approach Blaenavon. Use Junction 25A if using the M4 from the East, or Junction 26 from the West. Head for Pontypool. From the Midlands use the M50, A40 then A465 to Brynmawr. From North & West Wales consider using the 'Heads of the Valleys' A465 to Brynmawr. As you approach the Railway, look out for the Colliery water tower – you can't miss it!

RAILWAY PRESERVATION SOCIETY OF IRELAND

Address: Castleview, Whitehead,
Co. Antrim, Northern Ireland BT38 9NA
Telephone Nº: (028) 2826-0803
Year Formed: 1964
Location of Line: Whitehead, Co. Antrim
Length of Line: ¼ mile
Gauge: Irish Standard

Nº of Steam Locos: 9
Nº of Other Locos: 5
Nº of Members: 1,100
Annual Membership Fee: Adult £25.00;
Senior £20.00; Junior £15.00; Family £60.00
Approx Nº of Visitors P.A.: 10,000
Web Site: www.rpsi-online.org
E-mail: rpsitrains@hotmail.com

GENERAL INFORMATION

Nearest NIR Station: Whitehead (½ mile)
Nearest Bus Station: Whitehead (½ mile)
Car Parking: Free parking at site
Coach Parking: Free parking at site
Souvenir Shop(s): Yes
Food & Drinks: Yes

SPECIAL INFORMATION

The Society is the only Main Line Steam Operator in Ireland.

OPERATING INFORMATION

Opening Times: Sundays in the Summer and also during Easter and Christmas. There is also a regular timetable of main line excursions. Phone for further details.
Steam Working: 2.00pm to 5.00pm at Whitehead
Prices: Depends on the event or the destination of main line excursions

Detailed Directions by Car:
Whitehead is situated about 15 miles to the North of Belfast just off the A2 between Larne and Carrickfergus. The location is clearly signposted in Whitehead.

RIBBLE STEAM RAILWAY

Address: Chain Caul Road, Preston, PR2 2PD
Telephone Nº: (01772) 728800
Year Formed: 1972 (at Southport)
Location: West of Preston City Centre
Length of Line: 3 mile round trip

Nº of Steam Locos: 22
Nº of Other Locos: 21
Nº of Members: 400
Annual Membership Fee: £12.00
Approx Nº of Visitors P.A.: 20,000+
Gauge: Standard
Web site: www.ribblesteam.org.uk

GENERAL INFORMATION

Nearest Mainline Station: Preston (2 miles)
Nearest Bus Station: Preston (2 miles)
Car Parking: Available on site
Coach Parking: Available on site
Souvenir Shop(s): Yes
Food & Drinks: Available

SPECIAL INFORMATION

The Railway's timetable is governed by High Tide on the River Ribble. This is because the line traverses a swing bridge across the Marina entrance – the only preserved steam line to have such a feature!

OPERATING INFORMATION

Opening Times: Open 10.30am to 5.00pm during weekends from 1st April to 30th September and on various other dates. Please contact the railway for further details.
Steam Working: On all days when the railway is open to the public. Trains run hourly from 11.00am to 4.00pm.
Prices: Adult Return £4.50
           Child Return £3.00
           Family Return £12.50
Note: Different prices may apply for Special Events.

Detailed Directions by Car:

From All Parts: The Railway is located on the Riversway/Docklands Business and Residential Park, just off the A583 Lytham/Blackpool road and approximately 1½ miles to the west of Preston City Centre. Follow the Brown Tourist signs from the A583 for the railway.

ROYAL DEESIDE RAILWAY

Address: Milton of Crathes, Crathes, Banchory, Kincardineshire **Telephone Nº**: (01224) 782479 **Year Formed**: 1996 **Location of Line**: Milton of Crathes **Length of Line**: ¼ mile	**Nº of Steam Locos**: 1 (Not in service) **Nº of Other Locos**: 2 **Nº of Members**: 250 **Annual Membership Fee**: £15.00 **Approx Nº of Visitors P.A.**: 3,000 **Gauge**: Standard **Web site**: www.deeside-railway.co.uk

GENERAL INFORMATION

Nearest Mainline Station: Aberdeen (14 miles)
Nearest Bus Station: Stagecoach Bluebird bus stop nearby on A93.
Car Parking: Free parking available on site
Coach Parking: Free parking available on site
Souvenir Shop(s): Yes – inside a static carriage
Food & Drinks: Yes – inside a static carriage

SPECIAL INFORMATION

The railway hopes to provide Brake van trips during 2006 over the ¼ mile of track laid thus far. This is subject to approval by HMRI. The steam locomotive 'Bon-Accord' is undergoing restoration at a private site. Realistic estimates suggest a 2007 arrival at Crathes.

OPERATING INFORMATION

Opening Times: A Café with light refreshments, shop and display is located in a static carriage and opens Saturday and Sunday afternoons 1.00pm to 5.00pm from May to September.
Steam Working: None at present.
Prices: Please phone the railway for details

Detailed Directions by Car:
From the South: Take the A90 to Stonehaven. Exit onto the B979 for Stonehaven and follow into the town square. Turn left at the traffic lights and follow signs for the A957 to Banchory (Historic Slug Road). Follow this road for 14 mile via Durris to Crathes and the junction with the A93. Turn left and follow the Brown Tourist signs, turning left for the railway after approximately 600 yards; From the North & West: Follow the A980 to Banchory and turn left onto the A93. Turn right following the Brown Tourist signs for the railway.

RUTLAND RAILWAY MUSEUM

Address: Cottesmore Iron Ore Mines Siding, Ashwell Road, Cottesmore, Oakham, Rutland LE15 7BX **Telephone Nº**: (01572) 813203 **Year Formed**: 1979 **Location of Line**: Between the villages of Cottesmore and Ashwell	**Length of Line**: ½ mile **Nº of Steam Locos**: 13 **Nº of Other Locos**: 26 **Nº of Members**: 150 **Annual Membership Fee**: £8.00 **Approx Nº of Visitors P.A.**: 8,000 **Gauge**: Standard

GENERAL INFORMATION

Nearest Mainline Station: Oakham (4 miles)
Nearest Bus Station: Cottesmore/Ashwell (1½ miles)
Car Parking: Available at the site
Coach Parking: Limited space available
Souvenir Shop(s): On operating days
Food & Drinks: On operating days only

SPECIAL INFORMATION

This Industrial Railway Heritage centre is located at the end of the former Ashwell-Cottesmore mineral branch and is based at the former exchange sidings.

OPERATING INFORMATION

Opening Times: Thursdays and Sundays throughout the year for static viewing. 11.00am to 4.00pm
Steam Working: 16th/17th/30th April; 1st/14th/28th/29th May; 4th/18th June; 2nd/16th/22nd/23rd July; 6th/20th/26th/27th August; 3rd/17th September; 3rd/10th/17th December.
Prices: Adult £4.00
　　　　　Child £3.00 (no charge for under 5's)
　　　　　Family £12.00
Prices are for admission to the site on steam operating days only. Admission is free at other times. Special prices apply to Santa Specials in December.

Detailed Directions by Car:
From All Parts: The Museum is situated 4 miles north of Oakham between Ashwell and Cottesmore. Follow the brown tourist signs from the B668 Oakham to A1 road or the signs from the A606 Stamford to Oakham Road.

Scottish Industrial Railway Centre

Address: Dunaskin Open Air Museum, Waterside, Patna, Ayrshire KA6 7JF	**N° of Steam Locos:** 9
Telephone N°: (01292) 531144 (Weekdays) (01292) 313579 (Evenings & Weekends)	**N° of Other Locos:** 26
Year Formed: 1974	**N° of Members:** 180
Location of Line: Dunaskin Ironworks	**Annual Membership Fee:** £10.00
Length of Line: A third of a mile	**Approx N° of Visitors P.A.:** 3,500
	Gauge: Standard
	Web site: www.arpg.org.uk

GENERAL INFORMATION

Nearest Mainline Station: Ayr (10 miles)
Nearest Bus Station: ½ hourly bus service from Ayr – phone (01292) 613500 for more information
Car Parking: Free parking available at the site
Coach Parking: Free parking available at the site
Souvenir Shop(s): Yes
Food & Drinks: Cafe on site

SPECIAL INFORMATION

The Railway is located at the Dunaskin Heritage Centre based on the preserved site of Europe's best remaining example of a Victorian Ironworks. In addition to the Railway, there are a number of other attractions on the site.

OPERATING INFORMATION

Opening Times: Operating days only.
Steam Working: Sundays in July and August plus the first Sunday in September. Trains run from 11.00am to 4.30pm on these days.
Prices: Adult £2.50
Child £2.00
Family Tickets £7.00

Detailed Directions by Car:
From All Parts: Dunaskin Open Air Museum is located adjacent to the A713 Ayr to Castle Douglas road.

SEVERN VALLEY RAILWAY

Address: Railway Station, Bewdley, Worcestershire DY12 1BG **Telephone Nº:** (01299) 403816 **Year Formed:** 1965 **Location of Line:** Kidderminster (Worcs.) to Bridgnorth (Shropshire) **Length of Line:** 16 miles	**Nº of Steam Locos:** 27 **Nº of Other Locos:** 12 **Nº of Members:** 13,000 **Annual Membership Fee:** Adult £14.00 **Approx Nº of Passengers P.A.:** 248,000 **Gauge:** Standard **Web site:** www.svr.co.uk

GENERAL INFORMATION

Nearest Mainline Station: Kidderminster (adjacent)
Nearest Bus Station: Kidderminster (500 yards)
Car Parking: Large car park at Kidderminster. Spaces also available at other stations.
Coach Parking: At Kidderminster
Souvenir Shop(s): At Kidderminster & Bridgnorth
Food & Drinks: Yes – on most trains. Also at Kidderminster, Bewdley and Bridgnorth

SPECIAL INFORMATION

The SVR has numerous special events including an Autumn Steam Gala, 1940's weekend, Classic Car & Bike Day and visits by Thomas the Tank Engine and Santa!

OPERATING INFORMATION

Opening Times: Weekends throughout the year. Also daily from 6th May to 1st October and during local School Holidays.
Steam Working: Train times vary depending on timetable information. Phone for details.
Prices: Vary depending on the journey taken:
    Family Day Rover £31.00
    (2 adults + 4 children)

Detailed Directions by Car:
For Kidderminster take M5 and exit Junction 3 or Junction 6. Follow the brown tourist signs for the railway; From the South: Take the M40 then M42 to Junction 1 for the A448 from Bromsgrove to Kidderminster.

THE SHAKESPEARE EXPRESS

Address: Vintage Trains Ltd, 670 Warwick Road, Tyseley, Birmingham B11 2HL
Telephone Nº: (0121) 707-4696
Year Formed: 1999
Location of Line: Birmingham Snow Hill, Tyseley, Stratford-upon-Avon

Length of Line: Approximately 25 miles
Nº of Steam Locos: 1 different loco each week from Tyseley Locomotive Works
Approx Nº of Visitors P.A.: Not known
Gauge: Standard
Web site: www.vintagetrains.co.uk

GENERAL INFORMATION

Nearest Mainline Station: Birmingham Snow Hill, Tyseley and Stratford-upon-Avon
Nearest Bus Station: Birmingham: Digbeth; Tyseley: Reddings Lane Stop; Stratford-upon-Avon: Stop outside of the station
Car Parking: 200 spaces at Tyseley site
Coach Parking: Spaces at Tyseley site
Souvenir Shop(s): Yes
Food & Drinks: Light refreshments on train

SPECIAL INFORMATION

England's fastest regular steam train runs on Summer Sundays to three destinations.

OPERATING INFORMATION

Opening Times: 2006: Sundays from July to September inclusive.
Steam Working: 10.30am and 3.39pm from Birmingham; 12.03pm and 4.55pm from Stratford-upon-Avon
Prices: Adult Return £17.50 (pre-booked)
Child Return £10.00 (pre-booked)
Family Return £39.00 (pre-booked only)
Single fares are also available. Pre-book or buy tickets on the day – group bookings are welcome.

Detailed Directions by Car to Tyseley Site:
From the North: Exit the M6 at Junction 6 and take A41 ring road towards Solihull; From the South: Exit the M42 at Junction 5 and take the A41 towards Birmingham.

SOUTH DEVON RAILWAY

Address: Buckfastleigh Station, Buckfastleigh, Devon TQ11 0DZ	**Nº of Steam Locos**: 16
Telephone Nº: (0845) 345-1427	**Nº of Other Locos**: 7
Year Formed: 1969	**Nº of Members**: 1,300
Location of Line: Totnes to Buckfastleigh via Staverton	**Annual Membership Fee**: £14.00
	Approx Nº of Visitors P.A.: 80,000
Length of Line: 7 miles	**Gauge**: Standard
	Web Site: www.southdevonrailway.org

GENERAL INFORMATION

Nearest Mainline Station: Totnes (¼ mile)
Nearest Bus Station: Totnes (½ mile), Buckfastleigh (Station Road)
Car Parking: Free parking at Buckfastleigh, Council/BR parking at Totnes
Coach Parking: As above
Souvenir Shop(s): Yes – Buckfastleigh & on train
Food & Drinks: Yes – at Buckfastleigh & on train

SPECIAL INFORMATION

The railway was opened in 1872 as the Totnes, Buckfastleigh & Ashburton Railway.

OPERATING INFORMATION

Opening Times: Daily from 25th March to 29th October. Also Santa Specials in December.
Steam Working: Almost all trains are steam hauled
Prices: Adult £8.80
  Child £5.30
  Family £25.30 (2 adults + 2 children)
  Senior Citizen £7.90
N.B. Extra discounts are available for large groups

Detailed Directions by Car:
Buckfastleigh is half way between Exeter and Plymouth on the A38 Devon Expressway. Totnes can be reached by taking the A385 from Paignton and Torquay. Brown tourist signs give directions for the railway.

SPA VALLEY RAILWAY

Address: West Station, Tunbridge Wells, Kent TN2 5QY	**Nº of Steam Locos**: 8
Telephone Nº: (01892) 537715	**Nº of Other Locos**: 9
Year Formed: 1985	**Nº of Members**: Approximately 660
Location of Line: Tunbridge Wells West to Birchden Junction on Gala days	**Annual Membership Fee**: £15.00
	Approx Nº of Visitors P.A.: 30,000
	Gauge: Standard
Length: 3½ miles (4½ miles on Gala days)	**Web Site**: www.spavalleyrailway.co.uk

GENERAL INFORMATION

Nearest Mainline Station: Tunbridge Wells Central (½ mile)
Nearest Bus Stop: Outside Sainsbury's (100yds)
Car Parking: Available nearby
Coach Parking: Coach station in Montacute Road (150 yards)
Souvenir Shop(s): Yes
Food & Drinks: Yes

SPECIAL INFORMATION

The Railway's Tunbridge Wells Terminus is in a historic and unique L.B. & S.C.R. engine shed. The Railway's aims are to extend to Eridge to connect with the Main Line.

OPERATING INFORMATION

Opening Times: Weekends from 25th March to 29th October. Some weekdays during School Holidays and also Santa Specials from 2nd to 24th December.
Steam Working: Most services are steam-hauled. Trains run from 10.30am to 4.30pm.
Prices: Adult Return £5.00
            Child/Senior Citizen Return £4.00
            Concessionary Return £4.50
            Family Return £15.00 (2 adult + 2 child)
Parties of 20 or more are charged at £4.50 per head.
Fares vary on some special event days.
Fares allow unlimited travel on the day of issue except for special event days.

Detailed Directions by Car:
The Spa Valley Railway is in the southern part of Tunbridge Wells, 100 yards off the A26. Station is adjacent to Sainsbury's and Homebase. Car Parks are nearby in Major Yorks Road, Union House & Linden Close.

STEAM – MUSEUM OF THE GREAT WESTERN RAILWAY

Address: STEAM – Museum of the Great Western Railway, Kemble Drive, Swindon SN2 2TA **Telephone N°:** (01793) 466646 **Year Formed:** 2000	**N° of Steam Locos:** 6 **N° of Other Locos:** 1 **Approx N° of Visitors P.A.:** 100,000 **Web site:** www.swindon.gov.uk/steam

GENERAL INFORMATION

Nearest Mainline Station: Swindon (10 min. walk)
Nearest Bus Station: Swindon (10 minute walk)
Car Parking: Ample parking space available in the Outlet Centre (charges apply)
Coach Parking: Free parking on site
Souvenir Shop(s): Yes
Food & Drinks: Yes

SPECIAL INFORMATION

Voted Wiltshire's Family Attraction of the Year, STEAM tells the story of the men and women who built the Great Western Railway.

OPERATING INFORMATION

Opening Times: Open daily all year round from 10.00am to 5.00pm.
Steam Working: During some special events only – please contact the Museum for details.
Prices: Adult Tickets £5.95
  Child Tickets £3.80
  Family Tickets £14.70
  Senior Citizen Tickets £3.90
  Children under 5 are admitted free

Detailed Directions by Car:

Exit the M4 at Junction 16 and follow the brown tourist signs to 'Outlet Centre'. Similarly follow the brown signs from all other major routes. From the Railway Station: STEAM is a short walk and is accessible through the pedestrian tunnel – entrance by Emlyn Square.

STRATHSPEY STEAM RAILWAY

Address: Aviemore Station, Dalfaber Road, Aviemore, Inverness-shire, PH22 1PY **Telephone Nº**: (01479) 810725 **Year Formed**: 1971 **Location of Line**: Aviemore to Boat of Garten and Broomhill, Inverness-shire	**Length of Line**: 9½ miles at present **Gauge**: Standard **Nº of Steam Locos**: 7 **Nº of Other Locos**: 10 **Nº of Members**: 800 **Annual Membership Fee**: £18.00 **Approx Nº of Visitors P.A.**: 56,000

GENERAL INFORMATION

Nearest Mainline Station: Aviemore – Strathspey trains depart from Platform 3
Nearest Bus Station: Aviemore (600 yds)
Car Parking: Available at all stations
Coach Parking: Available at Aviemore and Boat of Garten Stations
Souvenir Shop(s): Yes – at Aviemore and Boat of Garten Stations
Food & Drinks: Available on Steam trains only (except on Saturdays)

SPECIAL INFORMATION

The railway features in the BBC series 'Monarch of the Glen' and operates from Aviemore Station. In the waiting room, there is a small exhibition about the history of the line between Aviemore & Inverness and about the renovation of the station.

OPERATING INFORMATION

Opening Times: Daily from late May to 30th September. Restricted days in April, May and October and other dates in December. Phone for details. Generally open from 9.30am to 4.30pm.
Steam Working: Most trains are steam-hauled but diesel power is used whenever necessary. Phone the Railway for details.
Prices: Adult Return £9.50
Child Return £4.75
Family Return £24.00
(2 adults + up to 3 children)
Day Rover tickets are available for £12.00

Web site: www.strathspeyrailway.co.uk

Detailed Directions by Car:
For Aviemore Station from South: Take the A9 then B970 and turn left between the railway & river bridges. For Boat of Garten from North; Take the A9 then A938 to Carr Bridge, then B9153 and A95 and follow the signs; From North East: Take A95 to Boat of Garten or Broomhill (3½ miles South from Grantown-on-Spey.

SWANAGE RAILWAY

Address: Station House, Railway Station, Swanage, Dorset BH19 1HB **Telephone Nº**: (01929) 425800 **Year Formed**: 1976 **Location of Line**: Swanage to Norden **Length of Line**: 6 miles **Gauge**: Standard	**Nº of Steam Locos**: 5 **Nº of Other Locos**: 5 **Nº of Members**: 4,200 **Annual Membership Fee**: Adult £15.00; Junior/Senior Citizens £9.00; Family 30.00 **Approx Nº of Visitors P.A.**: 191,397 (exact figures for 2002) **Web site**: www.swanagerailway.co.uk

GENERAL INFORMATION

Nearest Mainline Station: Wareham (10 miles)
Nearest Bus Station: Swanage Station (adjacent)
Car Parking: Park & Ride at Norden. Public car parks in Swanage (5 minutes walk)
Coach Parking: Available at Norden
Souvenir Shop(s): Yes – at Swanage Station
Food & Drinks: Yes – buffet available on trains and also Swanage Station Buffet and at Norden.

SPECIAL INFORMATION

The railway runs along part of the route of the old Swanage to Wareham railway, opened in 1885.

OPERATING INFORMATION

Opening Times: Weekends throughout the year and daily from Easter to October. Also open on some other dates throughout the year. Open from 9.30am to 5.00pm.
Steam Working: All services are steam-hauled
Prices: Adult Return £7.50
　　　　　 Child Return £5.50
　　　　　 Family Ticket £21.00
Note: Day rover tickets are also available.

Detailed Directions by Car:
Norden Park & Ride Station is situated off the A351 on the approach to Corfe Castle. Swanage Station is situated in the centre of the town, just a few minutes walk from the beach. Take the A351 to reach Swanage.

Swansea Vale Railway

Address: Upper Bank Works, Pentrechwyth, Swansea SA1 7DB	**Nº of Steam Locos:** 5
Telephone Nº: (01792) 461000	**Nº of Other Locos:** 5
Year Formed: 1980	**Nº of Members:** 150
Location of Line: Six Pit Junction, Llansamlet, Swansea	**Annual Membership Fee:** £10.00
	Approx Nº of Visitors P.A.: 5,000
	Gauge: Standard
Length of Line: 2 miles	**Web site:** www.swanseavalerailway.co.uk

GENERAL INFORMATION

Nearest Mainline Station: Llansamlet (¾ mile)
Nearest Bus Station: Swansea Quadrant (3 miles)
Car Parking: 150 spaces available at the site
Coach Parking: 3 spaces available at the site
Souvenir Shop(s): Yes – on the trains
Food & Drinks: Light snacks are available on trains

SPECIAL INFORMATION

Guided tours can be arranged at £1.00 per head to view the shed, old turntable base and ash pit.

OPERATING INFORMATION

Opening Times: Services may be disrupted due to engineering works. Please contact the railway to confirm opening times.
Steam Working: Certain dates only, although most running days in the Summer are Steam days. Contact the railway for more information.
Prices: Adult £3.00
       Child £2.00
       Family £10.00
Pay once – ride all day.
Prices may change for special events.

Detailed Directions by Car:
From the East: Exit the M4 at Junction 44 (Swansea East), follow signs for Llansamlet and Morriston. At the third set of traffic lights turn left and look for the steam loco signs; From the West: Exit the M4 at Junction 45 (Morriston) then follow signs for Llansamlet; From City Centre: Cross the river near Parc Tawe Shopping Centre, follow signs to Llansamlet on A4217 for 3 miles. Pass the Colliers Arms on the left, pass under the main line railway bridge and turn next left.

SWINDON & CRICKLADE RAILWAY

Address: Blunsdon Station, Tadpole Lane, Blunsdon, Swindon, Wilts SN25 2DA **Phone Nº**: (01793) 771615 **Year Formed**: 1978 **Location of Line**: Blunsdon to Hayes Knoll **Length of Line**: ¾ mile	**Nº of Steam Locos**: 8 **Nº of Other Locos**: 7 **Nº of Members**: 700 **Annual Membership Fee**: £12.00 **Approx Nº of Visitors P.A.**: 14,000 **Gauge**: Standard

GENERAL INFORMATION

Nearest Mainline Station: Swindon (5 miles)
Nearest Bus Station: Bus stop at Oakhurst (¾ mile)
Car Parking: Free parking at Blunsdon Station
Coach Parking: Free parking at Blunsdon Station
Souvenir Shop(s): Yes
Food & Drinks: Yes

SPECIAL INFORMATION

The Engine Shed at Hayes Knoll Station is open to the public.

Web site: www.swindon-cricklade-railway.org

OPERATING INFORMATION

Opening Times: The Railway is open every weekend and Bank Holidays for viewing. Santa Specials in December and other various special events throughout the year have Steam train rides. Open 11.00am to 4.00pm.
Steam Working: Every Sunday from Easter until the end of October and certain other dates – contact the railway for further details.
Prices: Adult £3.50
Child £2.50
Family £10.00
Prices are different for special events.

Detailed Directions by Car:
From the M4: Exit the M4 at Junction 15 and follow the A419. After the roundabout by the Little Chef, turn left at the next set of traffic lights towards Blunsdon Stadium and follow the signs: From Cirencester: Follow the A419 to the traffic lights at the top of Blunsdon Hill, then turn right and follow signs for the railway.

TANFIELD RAILWAY

Address: Marley Hill Engine Shed, Old Marley Hill, Gateshead, Tyne & Wear NE16 5ET
Telephone Nº: (0191) 388-7545
Fax Nº: (0191) 387-4784
Year Formed: 1976
Location of Line: Between Sunniside & East Tanfield, Co. Durham

Length of Line: 3 miles
Nº of Steam Locos: 29 Standard, 2 Narrow
Nº Other Locos: 12 Standard, 15 Narrow
Nº of Members: 150
Annual Membership Fee: £8.00
Approx Nº of Visitors P.A.: 40,000
Gauge: Standard and Narrow gauge
Web site: www.tanfield-railway.co.uk

GENERAL INFORMATION

Nearest Mainline Station: Newcastle-upon-Tyne (8 miles)
Nearest Bus St'n: Gateshead Interchange (6 miles)
Car Parking: Spaces for 150 cars at Andrews House and 100 spaces at East Tanfield
Coach Parking: Spaces for 6 or 7 coaches only
Souvenir Shop(s): Yes
Food & Drinks: Yes – light snacks only

SPECIAL INFORMATION

Tanfield Railway is the oldest existing railway in use – it was originally opened in 1725. It also runs beside The Causey Arch, the oldest railway bridge in the world.

OPERATING INFORMATION

Opening Times: Every Sunday & Bank Holiday Monday throughout the year. Also opens on Wednesdays & Thursdays in Summer school holidays.
Steam Working: Trains run 11.00am to 4.00pm (11.30am to 3.15pm in the Winter).
Prices: Adult £6.00
Child £3.00 (Under 5's travel free)
Senior Citizen £4.00
Family £15.00 (2 adults + 2 children)

Detailed Directions by Car:
Sunniside Station is off the A6076 Sunniside to Stanley road in Co. Durham. To reach the Railway, leave A1(M), follow signs for Beamish museum at Chester-le-Street then continue to Stanley and follow Tanfield Railway signs.

TELFORD STEAM RAILWAY

Address: The Old Loco Shed, Bridge Road, Horsehay, Telford, Shropshire	**Nº of Steam Locos:** 5
Telephone Enquiries: (07765) 858348	**Nº of Other Locos:** 12
Year Formed: 1976	**Nº of Members:** Approximately 220
Location: Horsehay & Dawley Station	**Annual Membership Fee:** £8.50
Length of Line: ½ mile standard gauge, an eighth of a mile 2 foot narrow gauge	**Approx Nº of Visitors P.A.:** 10,000
	Web site: www.telfordsteamrailway.co.uk

GENERAL INFORMATION

Nearest Mainline Station: Wellington or Telford Central

Nearest Bus Station: Dawley (1 mile)

Car Parking: Free parking at the site

Coach Parking: Free parking at the site

Souvenir Shop(s): 'Freight Stop Gift Shop'

Food & Drinks: 'The Furnaces' Tea Room

SPECIAL INFORMATION

Telford Steam Railway has both a Standard Gauge and Narrow Gauge line as well as Miniature and Model Railways.

OPERATING INFORMATION

Opening Times: Every Sunday and Bank Holiday between Easter and the end of September. Santa Specials run in December. Open 11.00am to 4.30pm. Also open for static viewing on Saturdays from March to September.

Steam Working: 2 foot gauge on all operating days. Standard gauge on the last Sunday of the month, every Sunday in August and also on Bank Holidays.

Prices: Adult all day tickets £4.00
         Child all day tickets £2.00

Detailed Directions by Car:
From All Parts: Exit the M54 at Junction 6, travel south along the A5223 then follow the brown tourist signs for the railway.

TYSELEY LOCOMOTIVE WORKS VISITOR CENTRE

Address: 670 Warwick Road, Tyseley, Birmingham   B11 2HL
Telephone Nº: (0121) 707-4696
Year Formed: 1969
Location of Museum: Tyseley
Length of Line: A third of a mile

Nº of Steam Locos: Varies with visiting Locos and restoration contracts
Nº of Members: Approximately 600
Approx Nº of Visitors P.A.: 15,000
Gauge: Standard
Web site: www.vintagetrains.co.uk

GENERAL INFORMATION

Nearest Mainline Station: Tyseley (5 mins. walk)
Nearest Bus Station: Birmingham. Bus Stop at Reddings Lane – 2 minutes walk (Bus route 37 passes the entrance)
Car Parking: 200 spaces at Railway site
Coach Parking: Space at Railway site
Souvenir Shop(s): Yes
Food & Drinks: Yes

SPECIAL INFORMATION

The Museum runs a large workshop which produces refurbished locomotives.

OPERATING INFORMATION

Opening Times: Bank Holidays and Weekends only. Open from 10.00am to 4.00pm in the Winter, 10.00am to 5.00pm in the Summer.
Prices: Adult £2.50
Child £1.25
Family £6.25

Detailed Directions by Car:
From the North: Exit the M6 at Junction 6 and take A41 ring road towards Solihull; From the South: Exit the M42 at Junction 5 and take the A41 towards Birmingham.

VALE OF GLAMORGAN RAILWAY

Address: Barry Island Station, Barry Island, Vale of Glamorgan   CF62 5TH
Telephone Nº: (01446) 748816
Year Formed: 1979 (1994 on present site)
Location of Line: Barry Island
Length of Line: 3 miles

Nº of Steam Locos: 5 (10 in storage)
Nº of Other Locos: 3
Nº of Members: 300
Annual Membership Fee: £10.00
Approx Nº of Visitors P.A.: 15,000
Gauge: Standard

GENERAL INFORMATION

Nearest Mainline Station: Barry Island (across the platform)
Nearest Bus Station: Outside station
Car Parking: Large car park (300 yards)
Coach Parking: Car park (300 yards)
Souvenir Shop(s): Yes
Food & Drinks: Yes

SPECIAL INFORMATION

The aim of the company is to portray the rich history of railways in South Wales.

OPERATING INFORMATION

Opening Times: Weekends from June until early September. Special events will run at Easter and other times throughout the year. Trains run from 11.00am to 4.00pm. Please contact the railway for further details.
Steam Working: Please contact the railway for dates
Prices: Adult £5.00
Child £3.00
Family £14.00
(2 adults + 2 children)
Note: Prices shown above are for Day Rover tickets.

Detailed Directions by Car:
Exit the M4 at Junction 33 and follow the brown tourist signs for the funfair and beach to Barry Island. The station is situated on the left behind the funfair.

WENSLEYDALE RAILWAY

Address: Leeming Bar Station, Leases Road, Leeming Bar, Northallerton DL7 9AR	**Nº of Steam Locos:** None at present
Telephone Nº: 08454 50 54 74	**Nº of Other Locos:** Various Diesel locos
Year Formed: The railway association was formed in 1990, the Railway PLC in 2000.	**Nº of Members:** 3,500
	Annual Membership Fee: £12.00
	Approx Nº of Visitors P.A.: –
Location of Line: Leeming Bar to Redmire	**Gauge:** Standard
Length of Line: Approximately 16 miles	**Web site:** www.wensleydalerailway.com

GENERAL INFORMATION

Nearest Mainline Station: Northallerton (4 miles)
Nearest Bus Station: Northallerton (4 miles)
Car Parking: Available at Leeming Bar Station
Coach Parking: Available at Leeming Bar Station
Souvenir Shop(s): Yes
Food & Drinks: Buffet carriage only

SPECIAL INFORMATION

Most services are via DMU and travel to Leyburn & Redmire tourist destinations in the Wensleydale Valley. Other heritage diesel groups also use the line.

OPERATING INFORMATION

Opening Times: Weekends only during the Winter plus other days over Christmas New Year. Open daily during the summer. Contact the railway for details.
Steam Working: Only during occasional 'Thomas the Tank Engine' events.
Prices: Adult Day Rover £10.00
Child Day Rover £5.00
Senior Citizen Day Rover £8.00
Family Day Rover £25.00
Note: Single and return tickets may cost less than Day Rovers depending on length of journey taken.

Detailed Directions by Car:
From All Parts: Exit the A1 at the Leeming Bar exit and take the A684 towards Northallerton. The station is on the left after about ¼ mile close to the road junction and after the traffic lights. By Bus: The Dales & District 73 bus route travels between Northallerton and Leeming Bar.

WEST SOMERSET RAILWAY

Address: The Railway Station, Minehead, Somerset TA24 5BG	**Nº of Steam Locos**: 9
Telephone Nº: (01643) 704996 (enquiries)	**Nº of Other Locos**: 13
Year Formed: 1976	**Nº of Members**: 4,000
Location of Line: Bishops Lydeard (near Taunton) to Minehead	**Annual Membership Fee**: £15.00
	Approx Nº of Visitors P.A.: 195,000
Length of Line: 19¾ miles	**Gauge**: Standard

GENERAL INFORMATION

Nearest Mainline Station: Taunton (4 miles)
Nearest Bus Station: Taunton (4½ miles) – Services 28, 28A & 928 run to Bishops Lydeard
Car Parking: Free parking at Bishops Lydeard; Council car parking at Minehead
Coach Parking: As above
Souvenir Shop(s): Yes – at Minehead, Bishops Lydeard and Washford
Food & Drinks: Yes – At some stations. Buffet and Dining cars on all trains.

SPECIAL INFORMATION

Britain's longest Heritage railway runs through the Quantock Hills & along Bristol Channel Coast. Ten Stations with museums at Washford & Blue Anchor.

OPERATING INFORMATION

Opening Times: March to December. Daily from May to September. Open 9.30am to 5.30pm
Steam Working: All operatings days except Diesel Galas.
Prices: Adult £11.80
Child £5.90
Family £29.70 (2 adults + 4 children)

Web site: www.west-somerset-railway.co.uk

Detailed Directions by Car:
Exit the M5 at Taunton (Junction 25) and follow signs for A358 to Williton and then the A39 for Minehead. In Minehead, brown tourist signs give directions to the railway.

OTHER RAILWAYS UNDER DEVELOPMENT

NORTHAMPTONSHIRE IRONSTONE RAILWAY TRUST

Hunsbury Hill Country Park
Camp Hill
Northampton
Telephone: (01604) 702031
Web site: www.nirt.co.uk
Year formed: 1974
Location of Line: Hunsbury Hill Country Park, near junction 15A of the M1
Length of Line: 1½ miles (when work has been completed)

The line is currently closed for engineering work. Members of the NIRT have been working for some time re-grading the line and re-laying track and are making good progress.

ROTHER VALLEY RAILWAY

Robertsbridge Station
Station Road
Robertsbridge
TN23 5DG
Telephone: (01580) 881833
Web site: www.rothervalleyrailway.co.uk
Year formed: 1997
Location of Line: Opposite Robertsbridge Mainline Railway Station

The ultimate aim of the railway is to reconnect Robertsbridge with Bodiam, providing a link to the main line for the Kent & East Sussex Railway. This would boost tourism in the Rother Valley area and help to relieve traffic congestion and pollution. Passengers would once again be able to link with mainline trains and visit Bodiam Castle and Tenterden without using their cars.

The completion of this plan is still some way off and at present volunteers are working on Phase 1 of the project which aims to introduce a diesel-hauled Brake Van service over the 600 yards of existing track.

THE KEITH & DUFFTOWN RAILWAY

Address: Dufftown Station, Dufftown, Banffshire, AB55 4BA	**N° of Steam Locos:** None at present
Telephone N°: (01340) 821181	**N° of Other Locos:** 3
Year Formed: 2000	**N° of Members:** –
Location of Line: Keith to Dufftown	**Annual Membership Fee:** –
Length of Line: 11 miles	**Approx N° of Visitors P.A.:** –
	Gauge: Standard
	Web site: www.keith-dufftown.org.uk

GENERAL INFORMATION

Nearest Mainline Station: Keith (½ mile)
Nearest Bus Station: Keith
Car Parking: Available at the Station
Coach Parking: Available at the Station
Souvenir Shop(s): Yes
Food & Drinks: Available

SPECIAL INFORMATION

The Keith and Dufftown Railway is an eleven mile line linking the World's Malt Whisky Capital, Dufftown, to the market town of Keith. The line, which was reopened by volunteers during 2000 and 2001, passes through some of Scotland's most picturesque scenery, with forest and farmland, lochs and glens, castles and distilleries.

OPERATING INFORMATION

Opening Times: Weekends from Easter until the end of September and also on Fridays in June, July and August. Trains depart Dufftown from either 11.00am or 11.25am until 3.50pm.
Steam Working: None at present
Prices: Adult Return £9.50
Child Return £4.50
Senior Citizen Return £7.50
Family Return £23.00
Note: Shorter journeys are cheaper.

Detailed Directions by Car:
Keith Town Station is located in Keith, on the A96 Aberdeen to Inverness Road; Dufftown Station is about 1 mile to the north of the Dufftown Town Centre just off the A941 road to Elgin.

THE WEARDALE RAILWAY

Address: Stanhope Station, Stanhope, Bishop Auckland, DL13 2YS	**N° of Steam Locos**: 2
	N° of Other Locos: 3
Telephone N°: (01388) 526203	**N° of Members**: –
Year Formed: 2004	**Annual Membership Fee**: –
Location: Stanhope to Wolsingham, County Durham	**Approx N° of Visitors P.A.**: –
	Gauge: Standard
Length of Line: 5½ miles	**Web site**: www.weardale-railway.org.uk

SPECIAL INFORMATION

Situated on a section of the historic Stockton & Darlington Railway, the Weardale Railway opened for passenger services in July 2004 but quickly found itself with financial problems and went into administration within a few months. Although still closed at the time of our going to print, the railway hopes to leave administration later in 2006 and resume services as soon as it is able.

GENERAL INFORMATION

Nearest Mainline Station: Bishop Auckland
Nearest Bus Station: Bishop Auckland
Car Parking: Available at both Stanhope and Wolsingham Stations
Coach Parking: Available at Stanhope Station
Souvenir Shop(s): Yes
Food & Drinks: Available

OPERATING INFORMATION

Opening Times: Not operational at present.
Steam Working: None at present
Prices: –

Detailed Directions by Car:
From All Parts: Stanhope Station is located in Stanhope, just off the A689; Wolsingham Station is located in Wolsingham, also just off the A689.

ALSO AVAILABLE –

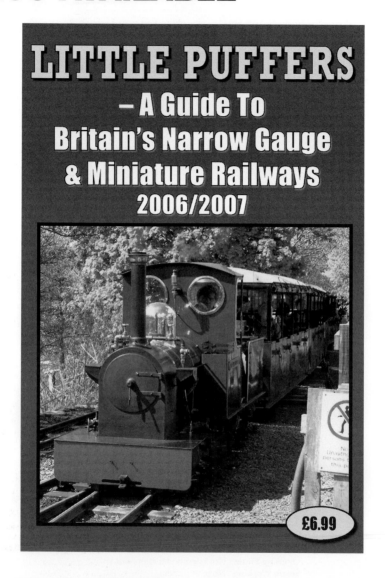

The new 2nd edition of **Little Puffers** is packed with information about Britain's Narrow-gauge & Miniature Railways and includes –

- **PHOTOS** • **DIRECTIONS** • **FARES** • **STEAMING DATES** • **CONTACT INFO**

…and much more. ***Priced just £6.99*** (UK post free)